SILVER LININGS

Prayer

Moments With God

Publications International, Ltd.

Cover illustration: Linda Montgomery

Illustrators: Vivian Browning, Marian Hirsch, Steven Mach, Linda Montgomery

Acknowledgments:
Pages 92–93: Excerpt from *The Collected Verse of Edgar A. Guest* by Edgar A. Guest, copyright © 1984. Used with permission of NTC/Contemporary Publishing Group.

Pages 98–101: Excerpt from *15 Minutes Alone with God* by Emilie Barnes, copyright © 1994, Harvest House Publishers, Eugene, Oregon 97402. Used by permission.

Page 119: Excerpt from *A Man Called Peter* by Catherine Marshall, copyright © 1951, Chosen Books, a division of Baker Book House Company. Used by permission.

Page 134: Excerpt from *Teenagers Pray,* copyright © 1955, Concordia Publishing House. Used with permission under license number 00:9-94.

Scripture quotations are from the *New Revised Standard Version* of the Bible, copyright © 1989, by the Division of Christian Education of the National Council of the Churches of Christ in the United States of America, and are used by permission. All rights reserved. Marked translations are *New International Version* (NIV) and *New Living Translation* (NLT).

Contents

6

Spending Time With God

8

The Power of Prayer

38

Teach and Guide Us, Lord

62

Praying for Others

82

Expressing Gratitude and Praise

110

A Plea for Help

138

Seeking God's Grace and Mercy

162

A Closer Walk With God

Spending Time With God

*U*nlike any of God's other creatures, humans have a deep desire to converse with their Creator. Whether we're happy or sad, thankful or needy, praising or questioning, we want to express what's on our minds and in our hearts to God. We seek to share what's in our souls with God because, as St. Augustine said, "Thou hast made us for Thyself, and the heart of man is restless until it finds its rest in Thee." We speak to God because prayer is our window to the architect of the universe and our lives.

Prayer: Moments With God includes stories, hymns, poems, meditations, and biblical verses, many of which are really prayers. They convey the immense range of emotions and thoughts that we have throughout our lives. We can identify with what is written in this book because at one time or another, we've all turned to God for direction or help, offered our praises and gratitude to him, or struggled with him about some vexing issue in our lives. For whatever reason we may need to go to God, this book will inspire us to be even more open and candid to the one who will surely answer us and give us true rest for our souls.

"Prayer is a powerful thing," said the sixteenth-century German reformer Martin Luther, "for God has bound and tied himself thereto. None can believe how powerful prayer is, and what it is able to effect, but those who have learned it by experience." In other words, until we pray, and continue to pray, we will never discover how prayer can affect our lives. God is deeply concerned about our spiritual, emotional, and physical welfare. *Prayer: Moments With God* provides examples and insights on how to  pray. It will show us that prayer is exceedingly helpful, necessary, and inspired by God. After all, our Creator wants to communicate with us, too. Whatever our circumstances, however we feel, we can always turn to prayer when we want to talk with God.

*Your changes touch
my life with hope and mystery.
God of love and power, I come
today ready and eager to
experience your power working
through me. Amen.*

The Power of
Prayer

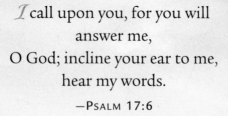

I call upon you, for you will
answer me,
O God; incline your ear to me,
hear my words.

—PSALM 17:6

*P*rayer is a participation in
willing God's will. While God's
ultimate will cannot be
thwarted, the strategy God uses
to reach that goal may be
infinitely variable. The prayers
of committed people become
part of the cosmic reality God
has to work with. God can use
them to "tip the balance" and
change the shape of distorted
reality in our world.

—MARJORIE J. THOMPSON,
*SOUL FEAST: AN INVITATION TO
THE CHRISTIAN SPIRITUAL LIFE*

Very truly, I tell you, if you ask anything of the Father in my name, he will give it to you. Until now you have not asked for anything in my name. Ask and you will receive, so that your joy may be complete.

—JOHN 16:23–24

Slowing Down

You heard my prayers to ease my
pell-mell race through life, and I am changing.
Only you could teach this old dog new tricks.
I feel your companionship in walks and
exercise, in contemplation and prayer.
I'm enjoying this new pace you set.

Hands of Prayer

More things are wrought by
    prayer
Than this world dreams of,
    Wherefore, let thy voice
Rise like a fountain for me
    night and day.
For what are men better than
    sheep or goats
That nourish a blind life within
    the brain,
If, knowing God, they lift not
    hands of prayer
Both for themselves and those
    who call them friend?
For so the whole round earth is
    every way
Bound by gold chains about the
    feet of God.

—ALFRED, LORD TENNYSON,
MORTE D'ARTHUR

Another Promise

*A*re any among you sick? They should call for the elders of the church and have them pray over them, anointing them with oil in the name of the Lord. The prayer of faith will save the sick, and the Lord will raise them up.

—JAMES 5:14–15

Listen First, Ask Second

As a child, I made up a Christmas list of things I wanted Santa Claus to bring. I dutifully mailed the list to the North Pole (I wonder what the Post Office did with all those letters) and expected Santa to answer my requests. I usually did get a number of toys at Christmas, and in the joy of the day I never remembered to check to see if I received all the things I had asked for. Besides, this was before computers, and I didn't keep a record of the list I had sent to Santa.

When I got older and found out that some-one other than Santa was reading and respond-ing to my list, I modified my requests. I began to ask for things that were likely or possible for my parents to buy for me. I knew that they would do their best, not only for me but also for my brother and sister. The content of my asking changed as I understood more about the true meaning of Christmas and the gener-ous love of my parents.

In our prayers of asking, our prayers of petition, there is a similar maturing process. At first, we may approach God with a laundry list of things we want for ourselves or for others. The only times we pray are when we want something. We keep talking to or at God. Such a diet of prayer may turn out to be more frustrating than fulfilling as we begin to notice that God does not seem to be answering. We are not even sure that God hears our requests.

Though God wants us to pray, he longs for a two-way conversation. God desires a deeper relationship. The context for our prayer requests is an ongoing relationship with God, who wants us to listen as well as to speak.

In the development of a child's language skills, listening precedes speaking. Children learn to speak by listening to adults. We learn to address God by developing our ability to listen to God, to encounter God in the wonders of nature, in the poetic verses of the psalms and in the stories of Jesus, in our dreams and in our encounters with people and situations of everyday life. We get to know God as we watch other people pray and live their lives as Christians.

I visited a friend who showed me a diagram of a hand. On each of the fingers was written a type of prayer. The thumb was labeled prayer of adoration. The index finger was prayer of thanksgiving. The middle finger was prayer of confession, and the ring finger was prayer of intercession. The little finger was marked prayer of petition for oneself. I liked the simplicity of the idea. I could be reminded to pray by looking at my hand and moving each finger. I liked a note on the paper that said if the first four kinds (or fingers) of prayer are well developed, than the last and smallest finger of prayer would be in proper perspective. Once again, I had discovered the maturity of prayer. We don't begin with prayers of petition; they flow out of a life of prayer that knows adoration, thanksgiving, confession, and intercession.

As we get to know God better, as we listen and speak to God, we will begin to have our prayers of petition shaped by our growing understanding of God's purposes in our lives. We give thanks for the way God has already worked in our lives and in the lives of those dear to us. We give thanks and entrust our prayers to the God who is faithfully and persistently working for good in the world.

Ask, Search, and Knock

I had just returned from a conference and was walking to claim my baggage when I noticed an older woman ahead of me, walking slowly and with some difficulty. Just as I noticed her, the young couple who had been sitting next to me on the airplane came abreast of her and asked if they could help. The young man offered to carry her bag, but she declined and instead moved between the couple and took hold of the young woman's arm for support. Slowly, with the older woman voicing her thanks, the three headed to the baggage return.

After retrieving my bags, I boarded a bus to go to the parking lot. Another young couple got on the bus at the next stop. I heard them remark about some roses that an older woman sitting near them was holding. The conversation continued in another language, and I did not pay much attention. Then I heard, "gracias," and I looked up to see that the older woman had given two beautiful garden roses to the young woman.

I thought if these people, strangers to one another, can show such kindness to each other, imagine the incredible, overflowing, loving intention of God.

Jesus used graphic images, ordinary experiences to contrast human generosity with divine generosity. If humans can give good gifts, show genuine kindness, care for their youngest, imagine how much more God will care for you. What we experience of kindness in our families and communities is but a foretaste of the great compassion of God, who hears us when we pray and is ready to respond to our needs.

St. Augustine once said, "Our hearts are restless until they find their rest in God." God has put a restlessness in us that keeps us asking, searching, and knocking. People are hungry for meaning in life, for something that lasts longer than the joy of the latest purchase or the most recent success. God is ready to hear our stories and open the door to a deeper relationship.

Asking is most often a verbal activity. We ask a question for information or direction. In our address to God, we ask for guidance, for help. We go to the one who can answer the difficult questions of life, who can show us love, acceptance, and forgiveness. God truly welcomes our questions and is eager for our interest.

Searching implies some movement and an awareness that something is lost or missing. If God has placed a hunger in our soul, a restlessness in our spirit, then we all are on a quest for the divine. This is not some search for an object, career, or feeling. It is a search for home, for the place where we dwell with our loving Creator. God welcomes our search and promises that we will find our home in God.

Knocking at a door means we wish to enter another room or place. There is somewhere else we wish to go or explore. God is waiting for our knock and is ready to open the door to a life of meaning, joy, and forgiveness.

Asking, searching, and knocking are wonderful images that beckon us to move toward God. God is ready and waiting for our inquiry. God put the very desire and hunger in our hearts, and he promises to hear our prayers, meet our searching, and open the door.

Serving the Dying

Many people have found comfort through hospice care—both the terminally ill patients and their loved ones. Even the nurses, doctors, and volunteers who provide hospice care often find their own lives changed in the process.

A friend who didn't drive asked if I could take her to the hospice volunteer-training classes she was attending. My first reaction was to think of the discomfort I felt around dying people, even though I'd been a nurse years before—their suffering unnerved me. But I decided to take the classes with her, just to see what it was all about. Soon I discovered there were ways to ease my discomfort around dying people, but even more importantly, there were ways I could help ease their suffering. The main thing I saw in the volunteers and workers who helped us in the training was that they cared so much about people—I wanted to care that much, too.

At first it seemed painfully difficult to go into a stranger's room at the hospice house where I've volunteered for the past 1½ years.

I would plead to God: "Show me what to do and say!" And he has.

I've learned many things from serving as a hospice volunteer. I've learned about dying with dignity and releasing one's suffering to God. I've learned how to be a better listener. I've learned how important it is to "seize the day," and even the moment—there are times I would say to myself, "I'll stop in and see her next time," and the next time wouldn't come because she had died. I've learned that even the little things matter—like a smile, a hug, holding someone's hand, reading from the Bible, or pushing a patient outside in a wheelchair.

I've learned about the power of prayer. One time a patient said, "I can't handle this anymore." I knew she believed in God, so I asked, "Do you want me to pray for you?" She said yes, so I did—out loud. God gave her peace and strength to make it over that hurdle.

I've learned that dying time can be a beautiful time, despite the suffering and uncertainty involved. I've learned how to mourn with those who mourn. I've learned about dealing with my own grief and loss and how to let go of self-pity, so I can cherish the act of living my life.

Serving with hospice has given me an education no textbook could provide. And it has changed me—for the better.

—A HOSPICE VOLUNTEER

A New Day

Everything looks much
brighter than it did before.
My prayer for strength has
been answered.
My cries for help have been heard.
My pleas for mercy flew directly
to your throne.
Now I'm ready to help
my neighbor, Lord.
Let me not delay.

*A*sk, and it will be given you;
search, and you will find; knock,
and the door will be opened for
you. For everyone who asks
receives, and everyone who
searches finds, and for everyone
who knocks, the door will be
opened. Is there anyone among
you who, if your child asks for
bread, will give a stone? Or if the
child asks for a fish, will give a
snake? If you then, who are evil,
know how to give good gifts to
your children, how much more
will your Father in heaven
give good things to those
who ask him!

—MATTHEW 7:7–11

*B*etween the humble and
contrite heart and the majesty
of heaven there are no barriers;
the only password is prayer.

—HOSEA BALLOU

A Mother of Faith

Sometimes a person doesn't have much faith in himself, but a loved one has faith enough to fill in the gaps.

Who could have believed that the worst student in Higgins Elementary School fifth grade would one day become a world-famous brain surgeon? That a poor ghetto kid would learn to perform operations too risky for some of the most highly trained surgeons to attempt? That the kid who got zero out of thirty on his math quizzes would regularly snatch the lives of tiny children from the edge of death?

Mother believed. She told me many times, "If you ask the Lord for something and believe he will do it, then it'll happen." My life is living proof that it's true.

—BEN CARSON, M.D.,
DIRECTOR OF PEDIATRIC NEUROSURGERY,
JOHNS HOPKINS UNIVERSITY,
FROM THE BOOK *BEN CARSON*

Our confidence in the power
of prayer is rooted in the
promise that God is continually
working for good in the midst
of ambiguous situations and
that God's purposes will
prevail in the end.

—MARJORIE J. THOMPSON,
*SOUL FEAST: AN INVITATION TO THE
CHRISTIAN SPIRITUAL LIFE*

Ordinary Miracles

*When we doubt your miracle-making power,
Lord, show us the ordinary miracles of season,
of hope regained, of love from family and
friends, and of surprises that turn out to be
miraculous simply by remaking our lives.*

And this is the boldness we have in him, that if we ask anything according to his will, he hears us. And if we know that he hears us in whatever we ask, we know that we have obtained the requests made of him.

—1 JOHN 5:14–15

The night is given us to take breath, to pray, to drink deep at the fountain of power. The day, to use the strength which has been given us, to go forth to work with it till the evening.

—FLORENCE NIGHTINGALE

Share a Prayer

Again, truly I tell you, if two of you agree on earth about anything you ask, it will be done for you by my Father in heaven. For where two or three are gathered in my name, I am there among them.

—MATTHEW 18:19–20

Shortly after Dallas Seminary was founded in 1924, the new school was threatened with bankruptcy. The creditors were going to foreclose, and on the morning of the foreclosure the founders met in the president's office to pray together for God's help in their time of need.

Dr. Harry Ironsides was well known for his short and candid prayers. Characteristically, he simply prayed, "Lord, we know you own the cattle on a thousand hills. Please sell some of them, and send us the money."

While they were praying, a man came into the business office and spoke to the secretary. "I sold two carloads of cattle and have spent the morning trying to make a business deal go through," he said. "It's just not working out, and I feel the Lord wants me to give this money

to the seminary. I don't know if you need it, but here's the check." Then he left.

The secretary knew the men were praying earnestly about the financial emergency they were facing, so she went to the door of the president's office and knocked timidly. "I think you should see this, sir," she said.

The president took the check out of her hand. It was for the exact amount they needed. "Harry," he said, "God sold the cattle."

This is only one of many remarkable stories that can be and are told about what happens when people pray together. Such stories were common in the early church, when, according to Luke in his letter to Theopolis, "they all joined together constantly in prayer." As the people devoted themselves to the apostles' teachings and to fellowship, to the breaking of bread and to prayer, "everyone was filled with awe, and many wonders and miraculous signs were done by the apostles."

In fact, the stories were so amazing that sometimes the people who were praying didn't even believe the answer. The Bible tells one story about early Christians who were praying for Peter to be released from prison, and when the maid came to tell them he was at the door, they made fun of her.

A similar thing occurred a few years ago when a bar was being built in a small town that had always been dry. A group of people in one church were opposed to the bar, and they called an all-night prayer meeting asking God to stop the project.

Lightning struck the tavern, and it burned to the ground. The owner of the bar sued the church, claiming they were responsible. But the church members hired a lawyer who claimed they weren't responsible. The judge was amused. "One thing is clear," he said. "The tavern owner believes in prayer and the Christians don't."

But of course they should, because Jesus made a remarkable promise. If just two or three people agree on something (and that's pretty remarkable in itself), his Father will do it. These could be people gathered in his name, seeking his will, experiencing his presence—under these conditions the power of their prayers would be magnified.

We often think of prayer as very personal and private, and sometimes it is. But there is a synergy in shared prayer, and the whole is often greater than the sum of its parts.

It's remarkable but true.

Unity in Prayer

*P*raying together brings us together. When we gather in Christian community, God is with us, and suddenly we are not separate individuals but one in Jesus' name.

For me, the most powerful part of our worship service is the prayer time when we begin by sharing joys (causes for thanksgiving to God) and concerns (specific requests for God's presence and power). The congregation so firmly believes in the power of intercessory

prayer that even visitors sometimes raise their hands to share what is heavy on their hearts so that the gathered community can offer prayers.

On any given week, there will be persons lifted up who are ill, who must face the death of a loved one, or who are dealing with depression. No request is unimportant. All requests for prayers are lifted up as the community prays together.

In sharing our lives, we not only know more about each other, but we are bonded by the belief that God hears our prayers and responds. Even when the outcome is not what we want, we trust in God.

There is sometimes a palpable presence of Jesus among us. Other times, it is more like a warm feeling of being surrounded in love and understanding. But there is never any doubt that the risen Lord stands among us.

I like the image of hot coals that when gathered together continue to provide warmth. Separate the coals and they cool. Even the most independent of us benefits from community. God didn't mean for us to go it alone!

Crazy Love

The Hebrew title of Psalm 34, "Praise for Deliverance from Trouble," indicates it was written during a dramatic time in David's life. Dramatic in many ways—David was putting on a performance.

You see, David was on the run from King Saul. The king was jealous of David's success in fighting the rival Philistines, and he wanted to do away with this young warrior. After scampering though the Judean desert and foothills, David tried hiding where Saul would never look for him—among the Philistines. Eventually, he was recognized as the guy who had slain thousands of their soldiers (including the famous giant Goliath), and so David had to think of something quick.

He pretended to be insane. He drooled. He scratched at doors like a dog. Who knows what other antics he came up with? But it all worked. When David was brought to the Philistine king, he wasn't imprisoned or executed, just kicked out of town. King Achish stared at this pitiful creature and came up with one of the great lines of Scripture: "Am I so short of madmen that you have to bring this fellow here to carry on in front of me?" (1 Samuel 21:15, NIV).

Indeed, life was pretty crazy for David in those days. There may have been moments when he himself wondered whether this was just an act or if he really was losing his mind. But through all of it, as Psalm 34 shows us, he clung to the one thing he knew for certain: The Lord cares.

You can bet that when he was pawing the palace gates like an animal he was praying—praying like crazy, you might say. "Lord, get me out of this!" Verse 4 mentions his "fears," and we can be sure that the danger was very real and very immediate. One swipe of a Philistine sword and it was curtains for David, no matter how good an actor he was. He needed major intervention for Achish to buy this act. And that's exactly what happened. The Lord heard his prayer and answered it, delivering David from seeming certain death.

When your life drives you bonkers, remember that the Lord cares. When you find yourself paralyzed by fears, call out for help. Bring your requests to God, and he will answer your prayers. And you don't have to put on an act with him. You don't have to be pretty or pious, perfect or pompous. David was drooling when he launched his prayer for help! In whatever condition you find yourself, present your requests to God, and trust him to respond in a way that's best for you.

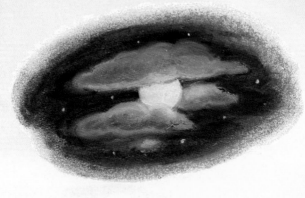

A Prayer by St. Paul

For this reason I bow my knees before the Father, from whom every family in heaven and on earth takes its name. I pray that, according to the riches of his glory, he may grant that you may be strengthened in your inner being with power through his Spirit, and that Christ may dwell in your hearts through faith, as you are being rooted and grounded in love. I pray that you may have the power to comprehend, with all the saints, what is the breadth and length and height and depth, and to know the love of Christ that surpasses knowledge, so that you may be filled with all the fullness of God. Now to him who by the power at work within us is able to accomplish abundantly far more than all we can ask or imagine, to him be glory in the church and in Christ Jesus to all generations, forever and ever. Amen.

—EPHESIANS 3:14–21

*God, you have promised me rest.
You have promised that
following you will be easier than
following myself. Today, please
teach me your gentle and humble
ways and help me rest in
your promise as I gladly
accept your guidance. Amen.*

Teach and Guide Us, Lord

A Family Prayer

*D*ear God, for our family we ask your love and care in the days and years ahead. We pray for the strength to go to work every day. It's not easy to get up early and then go out to face the world. The competition is tough, and the bottom line is inflexible. Give us the strength to work.

We pray for the health of each family member. You know our bodies better than we do. Every ache and pain, every sickness, is a concern to you. Therefore, we ask that you keep watch over our bones, muscles, and every bodily system, because you are the Great Healer.

We ask for guidance in all the decisions we must make in the days ahead, the big decisions, and even the little daily ones. We acknowledge that without divine direction, our lives become meaningless, wrapped up in our own selfishness, heading nowhere. Lead us where you want us to go!

Let us be friends with our neighbors. Especially give us patience when it seems our comforts are ignored or our rights infringed. In every dispute, let us be willing to be fair, and even take less than we deserve. And give us a spirit of humility that we might offer help and comfort when we see a neighbor in need.

For the students in this family, we pray for extended hours of concentration. We ask that the days of books and classes might be filled with energy and the joy of learning as you provide wisdom and intelligence. Give us time to play together, to have fun, and to laugh. For we know that your dwelling place is a place of joy and laughter. Let us experience a little bit of heaven on earth in this family.

Finally, increase the strength of our bonds of love so that we might bear witness to your love in our community. Give us the desire to offer hospitality at every opportunity. And throughout all our days together, may this family learn to worship better and better, seeing all you have so graciously given us. Amen.

I Am Listening

Lord, I want renewal in my life.
Please tell me what you want me to be, first,
then tell me what you want me to do. Speak,
for I am listening. Guide, for I am willing to
follow while I rest in your love.

New Direction

Life is full of trade-offs, Lord, and I need to make one. I want to venture off the fast track where I'm losing more than I'm gaining. Guide my search for a job where I can have both a life and a living. Restore my balance, not the checkbook kind, for it will change when I do. Your balance is not found running in a circle, but along a beckoning path where enough is more than sufficient; where money comes second to family, community, and self; where success takes on new meaning; and where, in the giving up, I gain wealth beyond belief.

God the Healer

*Please, Comforting Spirit, teach me
what it means to let go of the hope that others
will be my cure. You, Great Physician,
be my healer in this quiet hour.*

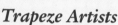

Trapeze Artists

*G*uide me, pathfinding God, for I'm an aerialist leaping from bar to bar. For seconds, I'm holding neither old nor new; it's impossible to grasp a second bar while holding the first. Parents understand. We can't embrace kids' growth while requiring them to stay the same. Help me teach my kids how to swing on *their* bars—have standards, goals, a living faith. Steady me as I help them soar, for holding them back says I think they *can't*. No matter what today is like, tomorrow will be different. Help me, and the kids, live gracefully in between.

So Little Time

S quare by square, we live our lives marked off in neat appointment-calendar blocks of time. Everybody gets only so much, no more, for the lines are already bulging. We pencil in commitments that spill over into tomorrow's squares. And just look at yesterday's notations: Nowhere did we get every "to do" done, every deadline met.

There is not enough time in the little squares we have allotted ourselves. O God, calling them life, we try to use a larger calendar with bigger squares, but all we do is schedule more. Our pencils eat up our best intentions for accepting your promised abundant life.

Help us, for we want to be more than just the sum of all we had scheduled, minus what we got done, multiplied by what we wished we'd been doing, tallied up to a bottom line of regret.

Guide us as we erase what is not essential. Forgive us for the day-squares where we've inched you out; our hectic dreariness reflects your absence.

Making New Places for God

Change is inevitable, Lord, we know.
Teach us to accept: If we view each transition
as an opportunity to experience your
faithfulness, then we make new places in
our lives for spiritual growth.

Friend in Need

We enjoy too much the superior feeling of
helping those in need. Teach us, Lord, that it
can be much harder to receive than to give.
And let us be humble enough to open our
own hands, too, when we're clearly in need.

Let Me Help

Teach me to really see with new eyes today—
especially the burden of care that others harbor
within them. Grant me insight to see beyond
smiling faces into hearts that hurt. And when I
recognize the pain, Lord, help me to reach out.

Dear God, teach me to never forget my true priorities: family, friends, and your will.

Teach us, good Lord, to serve
Thee as Thou deserves.
To give and not to count
the cost:
To fight and not to heed
the wounds:
To toil and not to seek for rest:
To labour and not to ask
for any reward
Save that of knowing that
we do thy will.

—ST. IGNATIUS LOYOLA,
"PRAYER FOR GENEROSITY"

Listening for God

Lord, we've tossed our prayers aloft, and hopefully, expectantly, we wait for your answers. As we do, we will listen, for you speak in the voice of nature; see you as a companion in the face and hand of a friend; feel you as a sweet-smelling rain, a river breeze; believe you can provide encouragement, direction, and guidance for those who have only to ask. We feel your presence.

Making a Choice

*L*ord, I read in a survey that more than half your working children, given a choice, parents would take more free or vacation time over more money. And it's true, as you know from our sharing concerns and frustrations with you, we are time deprived. These days, we would be happiest taking an extra day off work instead of the day's pay. Amazing!

Are the times changing, Lord? Are workaholics becoming passé and is prestige for working 20 hours a day dimming? Are we going to decide to have four-day weekends with more free time to spend with our family, friends, and you?

Probably not, Lord, for most of us won't have that choice right away. Most of us will remain secret "time-aholics," yearning in private for more time. Give us the wisdom to ask ourselves, "more time for what?"

Motivate us to answer in such ways that will goad us to find extra time now, for even an extra hour here or there would help. Even five extra hours a week would be enough time to . . . to what? What do we want to do so badly that we will give up a day's wages to do it?

Guide our search of current schedules to see where we can pluck extra time: mornings? late nights? weekends? Taking just a little from each one could give us a sizable pile of found time to use in new ways. Help us be satisfied with this small step even as we hunger and plan for more.

Urge us to pay attention to our need for more time, for it is a worthy yearning. We need all the time we can get. And at the same time, when we find extra hours, restrain us with a gentle hand if we are tempted to squander any of our precious time doing things that seem hardly worth the effort much less worth swapping for a day's pay!

Thank you for the gift of extra time however, whenever, and wherever we gain it. With your guidance, we will invest it wisely.

Grains of Hope

*W*hen trouble strikes, O God, we are restored by small signs of hope found in ordinary places: friends, random kindness, shared pain, and support. Teach us to collect them like mustard seeds that can grow into a spreading harvest of well-being.

*L*ord, when I turn to you and trust you, you are very glad. Make me glad, too, as I learn to share your joy in finding what you lost. Amen.

Grace for Our Feast

We gather around this feasting table, humbled by our bounty, Lord of abundant life; we have so much more than we need. We confess that we are poised, fork in hand, ready to overdo. Help us learn better how to live as grateful children—delighted, surprised, and generous with the sharing of our good fortune. Bless us now as we enjoy it amidst food, friends, and family. We give the heartiest thanks for your diligent, steadfast care of us.

What About the Kids?

Childhood is a treasure, and as working parents, we fear we're squandering it as we hire strangers to share and mold it. Guide our choices, Lord. Hold our children in your hands while we're gone.

Rejoice With Me

I spend a lot of time looking for things that are lost: lost keys, lost glasses, lost papers—especially lost papers. I'm a teacher, and I'm always making copies of interesting articles, stacking them in piles, and then placing them in files. Soon I have piles of files.

Then, when something comes up in class or in a project, I think, "Oh, I read something about that. Now let's see, where did I put that article?"

If it is important enough, I start sorting through things, and usually I can find what I need. Often I can do this in just minutes, because the things I remember best are closest to the top of one pile. And if I can't find it easily, I move on, anticipating the day when I will have all this organized. My wife, Katie, is pretty certain such a day will never come, but she is the kind of person who always puts her glasses in the same place.

Sometimes, however, I need a specific piece of information, and I will spend days looking for it. I realize this is not a good use of my time. But what I am looking for is often the piece

I need to finish an article or make a case for a new program at school.

Often, when Katie calls to ask what I'm doing, I have to tell her, "I'm looking for the article I need." She is a nice person, so she doesn't say, "If you'd figure out how to keep a filing system, you wouldn't be wasting your life like this." Instead, she says, "I'll pray that you will find it," and she does.

Later, when I find what I need, I call her back, and she's glad for me. But she's never as glad as I am. That's because when I lose something important, it becomes even more important to me. And the more important it is, the happier I am when I find it.

Jesus knew this was true, and he told his disciples about a woman who had ten silver coins, but she lost one. There were few windows back then, and houses were dark. But the woman lit a lantern, and she swept the whole house looking for her lost coin.

These were silver coins, and it would take her a while to save enough to replace one. And they may also have had sentimental value, as part of her dowry, perhaps. If so, she may have worn all ten coins on a necklace, and her friends would have noticed immediately that one was missing.

So she searched everywhere, and when she found it, she called her friends and neighbors together. Then she had a party. "Rejoice with me," she said. "I have found the coin that I had lost." "Just so," Jesus said. "There is joy in the presence of the angels of God over one sinner who repents." Jesus told this story when the Pharisees accused him of eating with sinners.

God has lost something, too, and Jesus said he feels the same way when he finds it. He is willing to go to great extremes to find the sinners the Pharisees despised. When God finds one, there is a party in heaven. The angels

rejoice, and their joy is God's joy. In fact, God doesn't just smile, he sings. The prophet Zephaniah says, "The Lord, your God, is in your midst, a warrior who gives victory; he will rejoice over you with gladness, he will renew you in his love; he will exult over you with loud singing" (Zephaniah 3:17).

That's quite a celebration, and it must be quite a song.

Apart

Teach us both how valuable our relationship is during this time of separation. May we use the time wisely to consider our shortcomings, to seek ways to amend our faults, and to reconnect the relationship with a deeper love. Teach us to love each other in the same way you love us, for your love is generous, kind, and forgiving.

Answers

*W*e pray but don't feel answered, Lord. Help
us understand that regardless of the answers
we want, being connected to you through
prayer is changing us into "can do" people.
We *can* find solutions, we *can* try again. Looking back, we understand you did answer.

Binding up a Broken World

*Y*ou created your world as a circle of love,
God, a wonderful round globe of beauty. And
you create us still today in circles of love—
families, friendships, communities. Yet your
circle of love is repeatedly broken because of
our love of exclusion. We make separate circles:
inner circle and outer circle; circle of power
and circle of despair; circle of privilege and
circle of deprivation. We need your healing
touch to smooth our sharp edges. Teach us,
Lord, that only a fully round, hand-joined
circle can move freely like a spinning wheel on
the globe we call home.

Going for the Interview

I have an interview today, O God, and feel
inadequate to the task, much less the job
I am being considered for.

First impressions count for much, and I
may not wear the proper clothes, have the
correct attitude, or express the perfect smile,
immediately losing an advantage. I may make
silly mistakes, blundering through facts that I
know as well as my own name.

However, Lord, with you at my elbow, I will
be at ease, competent, and pleasant. Interviews
are like spinning coins: They can fall either way,
depending a lot upon how we view and present
ourselves. Help us consult with you about that
beforehand.

No matter what today's outcome is, remind
me to look in the mirror *you* hold up so that I
can see a reflection of someone who did their
very best.

If nothing else, Lord, this interview will be
good practice for others down the road; nothing is wasted in your world, even bad interviews, which can be redeemed into training
sessions for future triumph.

Around the Bend

I'm getting a crick in my neck trying to see around the bend, God of past and future. I'm wearing myself out second guessing. Teach me to live in today, needing just a small glimpse down the road. No need to borrow trouble that may not be waiting.

Winds of Change

Spirit of God, keep teaching me the ways of change and growth. Like the wind, you cannot be tracked or traced. The breezes blow where they will: silent, invisible, and with great power. Just as you are working in lives even now. Let me know your calling as you move in me! Yes, whisk with your persistent prompting through all the windows of my soul, the dark corners of my heart.

A Little Means a Lot

O God, healing is going so-o-o-o slowly, and I am impatient and grumpy. Mind, body, or soul, this takes a long time. Teach me that recovery is a journey, not a hasty jet-lagged arrival. Bless me with faith to sustain me, step by small step. You do miraculous things with faith as tiny as mustard seeds that, in time, blossom into awesome growth. I hold that picture as I make mustard-seed progress along the road to healing.

For Our Family

May your eyes look kindly upon my family,
Lord, for we need your love and guidance in
our lives. This is a family that seeks to do the
right things—to work hard for a living, to raise
up children who will contribute to society, and
to be a blessing in our neighborhood. But we
know we need your constant help to do these
things. May we be filled with love and happiness—all of us who live in this home: by fulfilling our responsibilities, day in and day out; by
being accountable in all our actions; by giving
whenever we can, even when it hurts; by nur-
turing warmth and understanding among us.
And by always looking out for the best interests
of others. Please grant our requests according
to your great goodness. Amen.

Is It Me?

Why can't we seem to get along, Lord?
Is it me? For a few moments, I will just
be silent . . . to listen for your answer.

Lord Jesus, go with me today.
Give me your power each step
   of the way.
Let your presence permeate my
   work and my play.
Lord Jesus, go with me today.
Lord Jesus, be with me
   tomorrow.
Heighten delight and diminish
   my sorrow,
And yet, where you lead, my dear
   Lord, I will follow—
Even if some things I find hard
   to accept.
Jesus, be with me tomorrow.

*Be with me now, Lord, as I leave not only a
familiar place, but a familiar me. Grant me
wisdom to go forward now, toward a new
home and life, solitary but free. Be with me,
for the way home has never seemed longer.*

At Home

$\mathcal{P}$rayer is needed for children and in families. Love begins at home and that is why it is important to pray together. If you pray together you will stay together and love each other as God loves each one of you.

—MOTHER TERESA OF CALCUTTA,
A SIMPLE PATH

Praying for Others

Bless my family, Lord. They are gifts from you,
evidence of your unwillingness for me to be
alone. Until I see you face to face, the faces of
those I love will be to me as your own.

For the Children

Bless these children, God. Keep them growing
in mind and body. Keep them ever moving and
reaching out toward the objects of their curios-
ity. And may they find, in all their explorations,
the one thing that holds them together: your
enduring love.

Rehearsal Dinner Grace:
A Prayer for Beginnings

*W*elcome to our party, Lord. Stand with us as we honor two special people poised at the edge of a great venture. Be with them on this, the final eve of their separateness, for soon they will become one. Be present at their daily table as you are with them around this festive banquet now. Be with us, too, their friends and family, as we share a meal, a memory, and a toast for new beginnings.

Wedding Blessing

*B*less the couple before you, Lord, with the best marriage has to share: peace, not of a stagnant pond, but of flowing rivers; strength, not of sheltered dogwood, but of oak, sycamore, and beech, deeply rooted and firmly resisting seasonal storms; power, not of fists and temper, but of growing branches stretching toward the sun.

Learning About Faith From Children

When someone, especially an expert, predicts the worst, we tend to believe him or her. It takes a dynamic faith to believe something different—to believe that God can and will intervene in the situation. This true story tells of a child who had that kind of faith.

"Let's pray together for Riffy," I said to my daughter, Tami, who was six years old.

I took our frail cat into my arms and stroked his caramel-colored fur. The doctor had told us there was no hope. The unknown infection, unresponsive to medication, was taking over Riffy's body. His fever remained high, his appetite low. The doctor said we could bring him home, but the symptoms would worsen. Then we could bring him back to be put to sleep.

I prepared in my mind a prayer about helping Tami deal with his inevitable death, but before I could get my prayer out, Tami began, "Oh God, we know you have great power. Please make Riffy all better, because he is my best friend. Amen."

Now we have a problem, I thought. I tried to say the prayer I had planned about preparing for Riffy's death, but Tami would have none of it. "God is going to make Riffy well, Mommy," she insisted. "I know he wouldn't take my best friend away from me."

How could I explain to her that God did not always heal? How could I explain God's sovereign plan, which we did not always understand? How could I explain the statement: "If it be thy will?"

I did not argue with her. I marveled at her faith (or was it naivete?). Worrisome thoughts about what was going to happen when Riffy's condition worsened nagged at me.

"Don't worry, Mom—Riffy will get better soon," she assured me.

Riffy did get well. The day after Tami's prayer, he started eating again. Purring and playing came next, and before long—much to our amazement (my husband's and mine and the doctor's)—Riffy was back to his frisky self again. Once again he hid under Tami's bed to jump out and bite our toes. He chased rodents in the yard and sometimes generously delivered them to our front door. And he resumed his regular adventure of climbing the tall pine tree in our back yard.

The only one who wasn't amazed by Riffy's recovery was Tami. She had faith all along.

Let Me Be a Healer

I wish to extend my love, Lord. So give me hands quick to work on behalf of the weak. Cause my feet to move swiftly in aid of the needy. Let my mouth speak words of encouragement and new life. And give my heart an ever-deepening joy through it all.

For All of Us

Bless mother and father, sister and brother, grandpa and grandma, uncle and aunt, and all the cousins. Here we are in your sight, this family: May we please you, day by day.

What to Do?

Someone I care about is suffering, Lord, and I feel helpless. Assure me that a little means a lot and that I'm sharing your healing love in my notes and visits. If you need me to do more, send me. I am like a dandelion seed, small but mighty in possibility.

Lord, I often pray for others when I need to pray with others. Show me the power of shared prayer as I meet with others in your name and in your presence. Amen.

For Everyone in Times of Trouble

O Lord, hear my prayer for all who are in trouble this day.

Comfort those who are facing the loss of a loved one. After the wrenching grief, let their lonely hours be filled with fond memories of days gone by. Also comfort those who are passing their days without work. During this time of financial stress, give them energy to make their employment the job of finding new work.

Encourage those who are finding it difficult to believe in the future. Let your hope fill their hearts as they recall all your past faithfulness. Though doubting the truth of your existence or the validity of your promises, bring wise friends into their lives who have long known the reality of your love. While they struggle to make ends meet, please let them be assured that you can take care of every need, no matter how large or small.

Heal those who are suffering pain and illness. Let them find rest and calm as they seek to make the idle moments pass more quickly. While they are racked in mind and stressed out emotionally, cradle their minds in your love and soothe every irrational thought that seeks to run out of control.

Uphold those who are being tempted in any way today, especially those who may want to end their lives. Show them that while there is life, there is hope, that change is the only constant, and that change for the better is so likely. Looking at all the negative aspects of life and finding it depressing, may they find joy in just one moment at a time. And may that be enough for now.

In all these ways, I ask your blessing upon those who are in trouble.

And please include me in that blessing, as well.

Three Crosses on the Water

One Sunday, a very striking mother and daughter visited our church. In a conversation with them after the worship service, I learned that the young woman was a singer from another part of the country, but she had not come west to sing. Cheri and her mother had come so she could receive a special kind of chemotherapy for her melanoma. Her mother had rented out their East Coast apartment and journeyed with Cheri to be her support person. While they were at the hospital, one of the counselors said, "You both are going to need a lot of support for Cheri's difficult treatment. Do you have a faith background, some religious community that can give you spiritual support?" They were not regular churchgoers, but they had some church contact, so they agreed to look for a church in their new short-term community. Somehow God led them to our church.

Over the next few months, I visited them in the hospital and at their apartment. They were wonderfully talented and creative individuals, very artistic and musical. They were ready to try anything to help stop the spread of cancer. We talked of prayer and meditation. They changed their diet. They went to support groups. They exercised and surrounded themselves with beauty—in nature and in art.

Still, the cancer progressed and took its toll on Cheri. The mother had already lost two husbands and was fighting to keep her only child. At times she would rail against God: "How can you let this happen? It is not fair!" Other times she would plead, "God, take me, not my lovely daughter who has so much to give." Her prayers reminded me of the psalms, so passionate, so filled with feeling, and so anguished. Her love and will were astounding. I was awed at her strength. I held her when she cried and listened when she prayed. I shared her anguish. I added my prayers.

Cheri died while I was away at a conference. When I got the call, I felt my heart sink at the news. Her mother was flying back to the East Coast for the funeral, and she wanted me to come and lead the funeral service because she had no home church. I made plans to leave my responsibilities early and fly east. All the way there I wondered what I would say to her friends and relatives who were filled with such grief and anger.

I wanted to speak words of comfort and hope. "Do not let your hearts be troubled. Whatever feelings you have, acknowledge them but do not let them dominate your heart. Do not lose sight of the joy in Cheri's life. Do not lose touch with a God who is bigger than death. Do not let your feelings obscure the compassion you can show to one another now and every day. Believe in God."

I tried to point them in the direction of God. I wanted them to look up from death and see the comfort God promises. The apostle John talked about the rooms that God has prepared for us—for Cheri. I hoped they would not let death rob them of their belief in God, who sustains us in life and in death. It was one of the hardest sermons I have ever given. I know the mother was grateful for my message, but she still had so many doubts after three significant loses.

Many months later, I learned the mother was back west to settle the closing of the apartment. I spoke with her, and she told me that the night before she had looked out the apartment window and had seen some boats in the ocean, fishing at night. When she looked back several minutes later, she saw three lighted

crosses, whose beams shone across the water right into her room. She thought of the crucifixion story. I asked her about the three deaths in her life. She said she had felt a great peace wash over her when she saw the crosses. The first real peace since Cheri's death. I said, "God even uses the rigging of three fishing boats to send you a message. It seems that God is at work sustaining you."

Do not let your hearts be troubled. Believe in God. These words I continue to pray for her.

Our Prayer Is for the Sick

*B*ring your cool caress to the foreheads of those suffering fever. By your spirit, lift the spirits of the bedridden and give comfort to those in pain. Strengthen all entrusted with the care of the infirm today, and give them renewed energy for their tasks. And remind us all that heaven awaits—where we will all be whole and healthy before you as brothers and sisters forever.

Blessings on the Anniversary Couple

*T*here is no greater mystery than love, Lord of covenants and promises. We are in its presence on this anniversary day. Bless those who live, day after day after ordinary day, within the fullness of married love, surely one of the greatest mysteries. Bless them as they honor their past, even while they create a future. Let them bask in the pleasures and applause of today, when we bow before their accomplishments, which, like the rings we read on the inner souls of trees, are an inspiration and blessing to us all.

Grace for the First Day of School

We've brought this child sitting across the breakfast table as far as we can go alone, Lord. Now we must share the pleasure, and the task, with others. Be with us, for it is hard to stand aside, opening the door upon a world of knowledge, peers, and farewells where parents can't go. Bless this special explorer; may your ever-vigilant love support and nurture this young mind just as the food before us now does the body. Rejoin us at supper tonight, Lord, for we'll have much to share with you.

The Biblical Theme of Forgiveness

*B*ecause none of us will ever be able to live a perfect life, we need to be understanding and practice forgiveness in our daily lives. Forgiveness is a theme that runs throughout

the pages of the Bible. When we confess our sins to Jesus Christ, we are promised that he will forgive (1 John 1:9). Then, in the Lord's Prayer, we are instructed to forgive others just as Christ forgave us (Matthew 6:12).

To forgive is to pardon completely and to forget the offense forever, without holding a grudge and without maintaining an attitude of condescending superiority because of what we have done.

There are times when every human being loses control. We explode in anger, say things that should not have been said, gossip, harbor jealousy or envy . . . or otherwise give in to subtle temptations. Sometimes we admit these tendencies, at least to ourselves, and recognize the presence of guilt because of our thoughts or actions. At other times we pretend to "have it all together" and walk about like the Pharisees of old claiming to be something that we are not . . .

Whenever we lose control or slip into sin, we can confess directly to God and know for certain that he will forgive without requiring that we do anything to atone for our wrongdoing.

At times, however, there can be value in confessing not only to God but to our fellow human beings. One way to care for others is to confess to one another, pray for one another, forgive one another, and accept each other with all of our human imperfections (James 5:16; Ephesians 4:32; Romans 15:7). Since God is clearly willing to forgive, we have a responsibility to do the same.

—GARY R. COLLINS, *THE JOY OF CARING*

Pray for One Another

People can often sense when someone is in need of prayer—even if that someone is miles away. If the thought of a friend should come into your mind, why not stop to say a little prayer on their behalf?

I cannot tell why there should
    come to me
A thought of someone miles and
    miles away,
In swift insistence on the
    memory,
Unless a need there be that I
    should pray.
Too hurried oft are we to spare
    the thought
For days together, of some friend
    away;
Perhaps God does it for us, and
    we ought
To read this signal as a call
    to pray.

Perhaps, just then, my friend has
    fiercer fight
And more appalling weakness,
    and decay
Of courage, darkness, some lost
    sense of right
And so in case he needs my
    prayer, I pray.
Friend, do the same for me.
    If I intrude
Unasked upon you, on some
    crowded day,
Give me a moment's prayer as
    interlude;
Be very sure I need it; therefore
    pray.

—MARIANNE FARNINGHAM

Lord, thank you for being
a God of new beginnings.
Give me a fresh start today
as I trust in you.

Expressing Gratitude and Praise

Praise to the Lord, the Almighty.
Praise to the Lord reigning;
  above all things so
  wondrously,
Shelt'ring you under his wings,
  and so gently sustaining!
Have you not seen all that is
  needful have been sent by his
  gracious ordaining?

—Joachim Neander

Lord, I am glad to be your child.
Thank you for your Holy Spirit, who watches
over me. Keep me safe until you come for me,
just as you promised. Amen.

*L*ord, thank you for listening to me and
watching me, even when I am alone and lost in
the desert. Give me peace as I trust in your
promises, and give me not just a drink of water
but a well of everlasting life. Amen.

Sing Praise for Today

May you celebrate this day with all your heart. Rejoice in the beauty of its light and warmth. Give thanks for the air and grass and sidewalks. Let gratitude for other faces flow into your soul. And cherish the chance to work and play, to think and speak—knowing this: All simple pleasures are opportunities for praise.

In Good Times

Bless us in this time of good fortune. Give us the grace to be grateful for newfound comforts, magnanimous among those who have less, and thoroughly giving with all we've been given.

Small Miracles

Praise you, Lord! The heavens declare your glory; the skies proclaim your mighty power. And here I am, looking up into those vast regions, knowing that the tiniest cell in my body is a most glorious miracle, as well. Praise you, Lord!

Our Prayer for Earth

For clean air and pure water; for glorious colors in sky and tree in first and last bloom, in the wings of migrating butterfly, goose, and bird, Lord of all, to you we raise our hymn of grateful praise.

For wildlife sanctuaries, open ranges, prairies, mountains; for backyard gardens; for corn stalks and bean stems growing tall then bending low for harvest; for your generous gifts that meet human need, Lord of all, to you we raise our hymn of grateful praise.

Every day and night we marvel at your wondrous care. Constantly, you guide our choices, inviting us to fruitful living. All creation reflects your empowering love: rolling countryside, stark canyons, majestic mountains, delicate wildflowers, and sturdy roadside blooms. Sunrise and star, warmth and chill—all declare your glory, singing together. Lord of all, to you we raise our hymn of grateful praise.

For love that gives us soul-satisfying happiness; for families, friends, and all others around us; for loved ones here and loved ones beyond; for tender, peaceful thoughts, Lord of all, to you we raise our hymn of grateful praise.

For letting us know you exist through families and friends who feed us more than enough food, who give us abundant shelter and clothing, and who cherish your presence and honor your creation, Lord of all, to you we raise our hymn of grateful praise.

For the pleasure of seeing your wonderful creation; for the pleasure of hearing other voices and music; for the delight of knowing and feeling; for gathering us in families and communities; for inspiring us to stretch toward new knowledge, heightened awareness; for the blending of all experience into the excitement we call life, Lord of all, to you we raise our hymn of grateful praise.

In Praise of the Usual

So much to celebrate, Lord: waking to dawn gilding trees; squeezing fresh orange juice, its zest clinging to my hands all day; making a new friend, talking to an old one; watching the first leaf bud, raking the last. Each day's turning brings gifts from you to celebrate.

Come, let us sing for joy
to the Lord;
let us shout aloud to the
Rock of our salvation.
Let us come before him
with thanksgiving
and extol him with
music and song.
For the Lord is the great God,
the great King above all gods.
In his hand are the
depths of the earth.

—PSALM 95:1–4 NIV

Telling the Family Tale

*Thank you for the gift of memory. Playing
"I remember" is such fun, Lord of history,
especially the sharing of it with grandchildren
who, like relay runners, are here to pick up
their part of our family tale.*

Longtime Friends

*Longtime friendship is a two-way mirror,
O God, a gift from you that returns our best
selves reflected in the joy others get from just
having us around. Thank you for the gift of
perseverance that keeps old friendships new.*

A Sense of Wonder

*In this beautiful place, there are wonders all
around me, God, I know. The only thing
lacking is wonder. Lift up my heart in praise!*

Pawprints

*W*inters can be long, Lord, as I've complained before, and hope elusive. Thank you for sending me outdoors. My spirit soars at the sight of a woodchuck waking from winter sleep. I rub sleep from my eyes, grateful for signposts of change, like pawprints in the mud, leading me to springs of the soul.

A Prayer for the Right Words

*T*hank you, God, for the wisdom to know
when to speak, what to say, and how to say it.
Guard my mouth today from any form of
foolishness, that in all circumstances I might
honor you with my words.

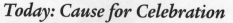

The Real Paycheck

I thank you for my work, Lord. Please bless me
in it. Most of all, help me remember that the
paycheck worth working for consists of more
than just money. It must include meaning and
significance, for myself and others.

Today: Cause for Celebration

*W*ith boldness and wonder and expectation,
I greet you this morning, God of sunrise and
rising dew. Gratefully, I look back to all that
was good yesterday, and in hope I face
forward, ready for today.

Circle of Love

*It is good, dear God, to be a part of this
family: circle of love, place of rest, bastion
of peace. When every other source of
comfort fails, this is where I return.
Thank you for being in our midst.*

For all the beauties of the day,
The innocence of
    childhood's play,
For health and strength and
    laughter sweet,
Dear Lord, our thanks
    we now repeat.

For this our daily gift of food
We offer now our gratitude,
For all the blessings we have
    known
Or debt of gratefulness we own.

Here at the table now we pray,
Keep us together down the way;
May this, our family circle, be
Held fast by love and unity.

Grant, when the shades of
    night shall fall,
Sweet be the dreams of one
    and all;
And when another day
    shall break
Unto Thy service may we wake.

—EDGAR A. GUEST, *GRACE AT EVENING*

Happy Anniversary

Thank you, Lord, for our marriage. Like a wedding band, our love encircles but doesn't bind. Like a vow, our love is words but sustains because of what they mean. In your grace, our love has the permanence of rock, not of walls, but of a bridge to moments ahead as special and bright as when we first met.

Morning

God, you are so great.
It is always the right time to
    worship you, but morning
    is best.
Praise for the dawning light
    that streams in through this
    window.
Praise for the sound of the birds
    as they flit through in the air.
Praise for the little spider
    crawling along the ceiling.
Praise for the smell of coffee and
    the warmth of a cup in my
    hands.
Praise for the flowering plant—
    and even those weeds growing
    by the house.
Praise for the neighbors walking
    along the sidewalk and the
    clouds moving by, too.

Most of all, praise for the breath
that keeps flowing in and out
of my lungs.
Yes, this is the greatest item of
praise: that you alone are my
life—all life itself.
Without you, all is dust.
Praise . . . for you.

Nourishing Tears

Thank you, Lord, for reddened eyes. Believing your promise that comfort follows mourning, we bawl and sob. In your wisdom, onion-peeling salty tears differ from cleansing grieving ones; we're grateful for their healing. Deliver us from stiff upper lips, and if we've lost our tears, help us find them.

Family Resemblance:
On Becoming a Grandparent

Thank you for the gift of ancestral faith. May I, as I take my place in the family portrait as the next generation, continue to keep you, everlasting God, as the centerpiece of our family, for your love is as ageless and steadfast as the wind calling my name. Watch over the grandchildren as you have over me in your special ways. Listen as I call out their names in echoes of those family prayers shared on my behalf through a lifetime of faithful love.

Thou, my all! My theme!
My inspiration! and my crown!
My strength in age—my rise in
   low estate!
My soul's ambition, pleasure,
wealth!—my world! My light in
   darkness!
and my life in death!
My boast through time! bliss
   though eternity! Eternity, too
short to speak thy praise!
Or fathom thy profound love
   to man!

—EDWARD YOUNG,
NIGHT THOUGHTS, "NIGHT IV"

Keep praying, but be
thankful that
God's answers are wiser
than your prayers.
—WILLIAM CULBERTSON

Tasting Steadfast Love

Steadfast love is a love that lasts, a love that is constant and enduring. You can count on this kind of love. Have you experienced this kind of love or at least a taste of it? It is a love that tells you something about God.

*P*arents can show some of this steadfast love. I grew a beard and long hair as soon as I went away to college. I was at a fine Christian college, and my parents had some images of what a fine Christian student should look like. They were surprised—actually shocked—when they saw me. It would not be the only time I made a choice that surprised or disappointed them, but they never ceased to love me. They were steadfast in their loving concern, while at the same time giving me freedom to make my own choices.

Longtime friends and loving spouses can also give us clues to this steadfast love. A friend who keeps in contact even though the distance is great testifies to an enduring love. Letters, phone calls, even e-mail have become the avenues of support and care. A spouse who knows our moods, who recognizes our short-comings, and who still loves us is a sign of this steadfast love.

These testimonies of human love are clues to the amazing love of God. Psalm 13 begins as a lament, asking where God is in the midst of pain and sorrow, asking how long enemies will seem to get the upper hand. The poet's concerns are poured out to God, but there is no doubt about the final outcome. God's love is sure. God's salvation is promised. God will act and give reason to sing.

When we see signs of God's love, when we feel like singing, we are entering a world of gratitude. Our lives become so aware of God's love that we find ourselves being filled with thanksgiving. We remember and respond to God's steadfast love with gratitude. In my journal, I keep a gratitude list. Each day during my prayer time, I jot down one thing I have noticed that I am thankful for. I give God thanks for the birds I hear singing, the roses in Mrs. Cain's yard, the good game my son played in baseball. The person who suggested that I keep a list said I should try not to repeat anything, that way I will sharpen my perceptions and look beyond the obvious. So I have thanked God for the smell of spring, the joke my daughter told, a long nap. It pushes me to see God's work in all the circumstances of life. We have even started to keep a gratitude journal in our home so all family members can add a prayer or note of thanksgiving.

Another response to the steadfast love of God is praise: "I will sing." I am not the greatest singer, but I know the value of singing songs of praise. To praise God in song lifts me to a joy-ous frame of mind. Forgotten are the lists and tasks still to accomplish. I am caught up in something larger than myself. I feel my whole self involved: my voice, the deepening of breath, the warmth of my body using energy to create music. I turn my focus from my particular needs to recognizing the God who is loving me and who is working for good in my world.

This is a good day to look back at all the ways God's love has been present in your life. You may wish to write a prayer of thanks, start a gratitude journal, or sing a song of praise. God has and will continue to love you and deal bountifully with you!

Father God, thank You for my
many friends who stand beside
me in all situations. They are
always there when I need them
to listen, laugh, and cry. They are
so special to my life. May they
realize what their friendship
means to me. Amen.

—EMILIE BARNES,
15 MINUTES ALONE WITH GOD

Grace for Advent

You are a welcome guest at this table, God, as
we pause in the midst of this bell-ringing,
carol-making season of too much to do. Send
us your gift of silent nights so that we can hear
and know what you will be bringing us this
year: yet another gift of hope. Bless our gathering around this table; we will set a place each
day for you. Join us in our daily feast, for which
we now give thanks. May it nourish our busy
bodies as the anticipation of your presence
among us does our weary spirits.

Lord God,
Your love is deeper than the deepest sea.
Your love is higher than the highest star in
    heaven.
Your grace to me is free—another unmatchable
    gift from you to me.
Give me thankfulness for your mercy.
Give me gratitude for your love.
Give me an appreciation of all your gifts—so
    freely given to one as undeserving as me.

In Thanks for a Good Day

How fortunate I feel today!
All is well.
Things are working out.
But is it luck . . . or is it your love?
I will assume the latter and offer
    words of praise:
Bless your name, Almighty One!

In the Blink of an Eye

*J*ust yesterday, the children were babies; overnight, they have jobs, homes, and babies of their own. "Overnight" change, Lord, is comforting, though, reminding me that nothing stays the same. Not tough times, not good ones, just the blending of one stage into another. I am grateful for the movement with you at my side.

Being Faithful

*S*ome prayers are best left unfinished, God of abundance, and this will be an ongoing conversation between us. Each day, I discover new gifts you offer me, and the list of reasons to be thankful grows. As I accept your gifts and live with them thankfully, guide me to become a person who shares with others so that they, too, can live abundantly. May someone, somewhere, someday say of me, "I am truly thankful to have this person in my life."

The Gift of Contrariness

Thank you, God of strong minds, for our bent toward contrariness. Created in your image, we are your stubborn children and proud of it. It takes a lot of backbone to stand tall these days.

When it comes to making life decisions, we don't want to be swayed by advice that comes and goes like fads of fashion. We confess to temptation because giving in and going along to get along are appealing.

Keep firm our resolve to be different; give us skills to handle teasing and taunts and temptation. Bless our stubbornness, our insistence from toddler days that "I can do it myself!" In your guiding hands, we trust that it is good—even essential—to live contrary. Thank you for the gift of intuition that bristles hairs on our necks and leads us to say, "No way."

And as hard as it often is, we will trust and follow you, even if it makes us look contrary. Sometimes, Lord, that simply means we are doing the right thing.

An Updated Portrait

*B*less my family, O God, for it is unique... some say too much so. I am grateful, for you know we are joined by love—for each other and for you. We are grateful you use more than one pattern to create a good family. This pioneering family has you at its heart.

After Loss, Going It Alone

*T*ime helps, Lord, but it never quite blunts the loneliness that loss brings. Thank you for the peace that is slowly seeping into my pores, allowing me to live with the unlivable; to bear the unbearable. Guide and bless my faltering steps down a new road. Prop me up when I think I can't go it alone; prod me when I tarry too long in lonely self-pity. Most of all, Kind Healer, thank you for the gifts of memory and dreams. The one comforts, the other beckons, both halves of a healing whole.

Caught up in Traditions

We're caught up in well-worn, comfy traditions, Lord. Keep them worthy, for like a deer path through the forest, they lead us forward and back. Thank you for the divine love and holiness found in the ordinary.

Great Physician

We don't really know why we have to get sick, Lord. We only know your promise: No matter where we are or what we are called upon to endure, there you are in the midst of it with us, never leaving our side. Not for a split second. Thank you, Holy One.

Gone but Not Forgotten

*The funeral flowers are fading,
O God, but not the presence of this special
one still with me in memory. As long as
I have it, shared time is not ended, merely
continued. Thank you for this gift.
It will make bearable the
solitary days ahead.*

But I trusted in your steadfast love;
my heart shall rejoice in your salvation.
I will sing to the Lord,
because he has dealt
bountifully with me.

—PSALM 13:5–6

Love diving, all loves excelling,
Joy of heaven to earth come
    down;
Fix in us thy humble dwelling;
All thy faithful mercies crown!
Jesus, Thou art all compassion,
Pure unbounded love Thou art;
Visit us with Thy salvation;
Enter every trembling heart.

Breathe, O breathe Thy
    loving Spirit,
Into every troubled breast!
Let us all in Thee inherit;
Let us find that second rest.
Take away our bent to sinning;
Alpha and Omega be;
End of faith, as its Beginning,
Set our hearts at liberty.

Finish, then, Thy new creation;
Pure and spotless let us be.
Let us see Thy great salvation
Perfectly restored in Thee;
Changed from glory into glory,
Till in heaven we take our place,
Till we cast our crowns before
      Thee,
Lost in wonder, love, and praise.

—CHARLES WESLEY

A Birthday Prayer

God of endings and beginnings, what joy to celebrate another happy return of my day. Give me courage to face what waits unseen ahead and what remains behind. At the turnstile of a new birthday year, I am excited and ready.

*In my distress I called upon
the Lord; to my God I cried for
help. From his temple he
heard my voice, and my cry to
him reached his ears.*

—Psalm 18:6

A Plea
for Help

God hears my cries for help, and
He answers every prayer.
I only need to be patient—
He supplies the "how" and
   "where."

Sometimes it may be immediate
In a tangible way I'll know;
While other times I wait assured
That he is strengthening
   my soul.

His grace is all-sufficient
To meet my heart-cries need.
As I lean upon his promises,
Walking in faith, he'll lead.

Lord, help me rest in you,
depending on you for all I need. And then,
Lord, please give me a harvest of joy.

Pulled Apart

Like the turkey wishbone, God of wholeness, I am being pulled apart by job, family, home, errands, friends, and my needs. I'm preoccupied with what I am not doing and feel the pull to do it all. Help me choose wisely. Remind me to negotiate on the job and at home for the time I need in both places. Remind me, O God, to negotiate with myself for a leaner lifestyle, for I am part of the pull. In the tugging days ahead, be the hinge that keeps my life's parts synchronized in harmonious movement, not split apart at all.

Hear my cry, O God; listen
to my prayer.
From the end of the earth I call
to you, when my heart is faint.
Lead me to the rock that is
higher than I;
for you are my refuge, a strong
tower against the enemy.

—PSALM 61:1–3

God Hears Our Cries

"Help!"—this is one of the simplest and most poignant of prayers. All of life is not peaches and cream or a box of chocolates. Life can be bruising and painful. Where do we go when things fall apart? Who do we turn to when darkness is all around?

The Jews believed that all of life was related to God. God was Creator of all the wonders of the earth, sky, and sea—from the beautiful rose to the soaring eagle to the mighty fish. As a Jew looked at creation, a prayer of praise and thanksgiving would be spoken: "Blessed are you, Creator of the universe, who brought forth this bread to eat on this new morning." God was praised throughout the day.

The Jews also believed that God was the Lord of history and was intimately involved in their struggle to be freed from slavery in Egypt, to find a new homeland that flowed with milk and honey, and to establish themselves as a nation obedient to God. History sometimes seemed cruel, and instead of happiness there was the bitterness of defeat at the hands of enemy nations.

As the Jews anguished and lamented about their problems, they took their complaints to God. After all, God was involved in history and would help them. The Book of Psalms is filled with prayers complaining to God about the circumstances of life—whether it be illness, famine, or losing a military battle. When things went wrong, the people prayed to God.

This prayer is in Psalm 18, which is in the past tense. The prayer then turns to thanksgiving: God heard my prayer; my cry reached the very throne of God; my anguish touched the heart of God. There is a wonderful confidence in this prayer that if God hears, then God will respond.

The psalms remind us that we, too, can take our complaints to God. The psalms coach us to pray and believe that God hears our prayers. "In my distress I called upon the Lord . . . and my cry to him reached his ears."

There was a time I was going through a difficult transition in a new job. I was working long hours and not taking time to pray. I ran out of energy. I prayed for help and direction. God's answer came in a letter from a friend. She wrote: "I suspect your greatest teacher will continue to be your own life with its ups and downs, its dry periods and oases. There is something very moving about that. It is so easy to speak of all the grand theories of spirituality; yet our lives often take us to another reality. That other reality shatters the ideal we constantly rebuild of a life full of great experiences of God. Those experiences are sometimes given. But I sometimes think the opposite experiences are the most important, because they bring us out of dependence on our mastery of the spiritual life and throw us in all our frailty toward growing dependence on God."

Her letter reminded me that I did not have to have it all together and that I needed to trust God. It is the simple assurance that God is with us, loves us, and listens to our prayers that really matters.

God is creative in responding to us, using the letter of a friend, a dream, a growing sense of peace, or a sudden insight. God hears and responds to our prayers.

Praying for Strength

O God … Help me to link
my littleness to Thy greatness,
my faintheartedness to Thy
loving aggression, my holding
back to Thy ongoings, my fear
to Thy faith—then nothing
can stop me. Amen.

—E. STANLEY JONES,
ABUNDANT LIVING

A Second Look

*Give me eyes, O God, to take a second look at
those who think, act, and look different from
me. Help me take seriously your image of them.
Equip me with acceptance and courage as I hold
out a welcoming hand knowing that you are
where strangers' hands meet.*

Not Overnight

Dear God, help me see that aging happens one
day at a time. Calm my fears that it will not
overtake and overwhelm me. Help me to
briefly mourn my youth as only a butterfly
cocoon that must crumble so that I may be free
as a new creature.

Prayer for Peace

When life's demands press in on us and we are weary in body and mind, we can call out to God for his peace.

Lord Jesus, as we pray for the Members of this body, its officers, and all those who share in its labors, we remember that Thou wert never in a hurry and never lost Thine inner peace even under pressure greater than we shall ever know.

But we are only human.

We grow tired.

We feel the strain of meeting deadlines, and we chafe under frustration.

We need poise and peace of mind, and only Thou canst supply the deepest needs of tired bodies, jaded spirits, and frayed nerves.

Give to us Thy peace and refresh us in our weariness, that this may be a good day with much done and done well, that we may say with Thy servant Paul, "I can do all things through Christ, who gives me strength." AMEN.

—PETER MARSHALL, *A MAN CALLED PETER*
BY CATHERINE MARSHALL

Peace in Our Home

Let your peace rest upon our
    home, dear God.
We do not know how to love one
    another as you have loved us.
We fail to reach out the way you
    have gathered us in.
We forget how to give when only
    taking fills our minds.
And, most of all, we need your
    presence to know
We are more than just parents
    and children.
We are also your beloved sons
    and daughters here.
Let your peace rest upon our
    home, dear God.

Calming the Storm

Help us as we weather this family conflict. We all have certain needs to be met, certain ways of trying to fulfill our dreams. Yet each of us seeks this one basic thing in the midst of it all: love. Simply love.

From Parent to Parent

Today I lost patience with my child. Please help me never to do it again, God. Teach me to see myself just as you see me: a learner still discovering life's wisdom, still experimenting with right and wrong, and still making foolish mistakes. Help me be understanding with my child just as you have always been with me.

Create in me a pure heart,
O God, and renew a steadfast
spirit within me.

—PSALM 51:10 NIV

*God, help me love you for yourself
and love others as you love me. Change me
as you love me and help me taste the
sweetness of your grace. Amen.*

God's Will

When life goes awry, Lord, I need someone to blame so I point the finger at you. Heaven help me, I want it both ways: you as sender and fixer of trouble. Help me know you don't will trouble, for what could you possibly gain? And when the good you want for me isn't possible in the randomness of life, I know you are always with me.

*I sought the Lord, and he
answered me,
and delivered me from
all my fears.*

—Psalm 34:4

As I go through this day, help
me to be sensitive to the fears
and cares of my fellow workers.
Remind me not to add my
grievances and burdens
to their own.

—ANONYMOUS

A Resilient Faith

*Even in our toughest moments, Lord,
we yearn to grow into the fullest flower.
Give us a faith as resilient and determined
as dandelions pushing up through
pavement cracks.*

Call to Action

We know, Lord, that action is the result of knowledge and spiritual insight. But so often we only want to think and reflect, without ever doing good toward anyone. Yes, it's easier to *know* the good than to *do* good. It's more comforting to be right than to do the right thing. It's more convenient to sit on the sidelines and give advice than it is to enter the game. It takes less energy to tell others how to carry their burdens than to take up a share of the load with them.

But we need to be shaken out of our lethargy, God. We need to recognize that our lack of love is evident in our lack of good deeds. We need to see ourselves just as we are: sometimes selfish, often lazy. Change us, God! Open our eyes that we may see the needs around us. Show us the poor—and all the ways we can help. Bring us to the sick— giving us words of comfort and creative means of helping. Let us no longer

pass by the hungry stranger, but move us to offer what is in our hand and in our cupboard.

Help us take the more difficult route of service. Help us forsake the ease and comfort of a purposeless life. Help us to be kind to the unlikable and to share with those who are different. Help us take all we know and put it into every resource at hand so that action may result for the good of all.

For if you will show us that we, too, are poor and hungry, feeble and needy in so many ways, then we will recognize that our giving can spring from what we have already been given.

Seasoned Workers

*W*hether we were ready or not, free time is at hand. Some of us are your finest seasoned workers, Lord, early retirees downsized, out-sized, and pushed out of our jobs prematurely. Help us start again, for we have talents other companies could use. Remind us as we start the search that you are searching with us. Keep us in the workforce, for we, like fine furniture, gain luster with age.

*My heart is broken, Lord, but I know you
can fix it. As I learn to depend on you,
give me the same thing you gave your
servant David: strength and a song.*

*Dear God, help me to love others
as you have loved me. Thank you for the
privilege of being your child as I love and serve
those around me. Amen.*

Imperfect

*O*nly machines run perfectly—for awhile—and we know exactly what to expect from them. But we are different, Lord. We often do the unexpected, certainly the imperfect. Give us the joy of diversity, the pleasure of indulging variety in our approaches to life. Being incomplete, we reach our hands to you, expecting help. And that is good, since only in you can we be perfectly fulfilled.

Giving In

*H*elp me remember, Lord, that I have not won an argument simply because my friend is remaining silent. I'm beginning to see that I have won nothing until I consider giving in. Help me do just that in this tough situation. I know it won't be easy, but keeping a friend is hard work. That's why friendship is such a valuable thing. And it's why I am so thankful to have it. Help me loosen my grip on this one thing. For the sake of my friend and for your sake.

Bring Back the Joy

How boring these meaningless
    details!
Is this really what work is meant
    to be?
Can you make it sing again?
Put the spark back in my zeal?
Because I know that work is a
    blessed privilege;
I don't want to be ungrateful.
But how boring the piles of
    paperwork,
how deadening the countless
    reports,
how fatiguing the endless round
    of meetings.
Yes, I need to feel it again, Lord—
    the joy of working.
Help!

Long Ago and Far Away

I was headed out the door when the phone
rang. The machine would get it, I figured,
but I paused to hear who it was.

"Hi, it's Faith," the voice crackled. "It's been
a long time."

Yes, it had. I had worked with Faith on a
project ten years earlier, and we had become
close friends. But she'd been living in the big
city for a year or two now, and we had lost
touch. She met a guy who distracted her from
old friendships. She stopped returning calls.

Now, after more than a year of silence, she
was reaching out over the phone lines. I had
somewhere to be. My hand was on the door-
knob, but her voice sounded so plaintive: "I
don't know if you want anything to do with
me, but I need some help."

I picked up the phone: "Faith, it's really
great to hear from you! I'm glad you called.
What's up?"

There on the phone and over lunch the
next day her story unfolded. The guy she loved
was indeed bad for her. She was basically
addicted to him, and he was addicted to drugs.
After being thoroughly used by him, she finally
broke off the relationship—and now she

needed strength to hold on to that decision. I agreed to help her as best I could.

When Faith called, she was in the place of the psalmist in Psalm 61. He was crying out to God "from the end of the earth." His heart was "faint." He felt very weak and far away from the help he needed.

Maybe you've been there, too. Your relationship with God used to be close, but you've been distracted by other loves. You've let your faith lapse as you've gotten yourself into more and more trouble. The tide of life has carried you out to sea, and now you feel as if you're a world away from where you used to be. Would God want anything to do with you anymore? Would he even know your name?

Some get to that point and never cry for help. They're too ashamed to pray, assuming that God would be miffed. But the psalmist assures us that the Lord listens to our prayers even when we're far away. In one famous parable, Jesus pictured God as a loving father watching for the return of his prodigal son. The father spied the boy "while he was still far off" and welcomed him with open arms (Luke 15:20).

Picture the high-powered executive who gets beeped during an important meeting. Checking the number, he excuses himself to

make an important return call to his daughter
at home, who needs help with her math home-
work. God is always on call. Sure, he must have
more important things to do, but he lovingly
chooses to attend to our needs.

So call him! No matter where you find
yourself, no matter how long it's been, God has
promised to listen to our prayers. He will take
your call.

Becoming a Friend

*I*t takes work to be the helpful, considerate, caring person that others will want to know and spend time with, but it is well worth the investment. Being a friend means that you need to reach out. Is there someone you can think of who needs to know that you are there for them—that you are a friend who cares? Pray for the spirit of friendship. So light up your life and radiate this brightness to someone who needs you.

"Dear God, shine through me and help me lighten another's darkness by showing the same friendship that you extended to me. Show me a person that is in desperate need of a friend today. Help me be sensitive, caring, and willing to go out of my way to meet this person's need right now, whether it be emotional, physical, or spiritual. Thank you that when I need a friend, YOU are the friend that sticks closer than a brother or sister. In Jesus' name, Amen."

Speaking Louder Than Words

Bless the words I am about to speak. And help me remember, too, that true eloquence does not consist of speech. Let me attend therefore to my character, for all I am speaks louder than anything I could say.

The Whole Package

Dear God, complaints sometimes come first before I can feel free to love you. Sometimes you seem distant and unreasonable, and uncaring. Help me understand why life can be so hurtful and hard. Hear my complaints and show me how to move through pain to rebirth.

A Prayer for Wisdom

Dear Lord, help me build a firm foundation by relying on your wisdom, diligently seeking your direction in all I do, learning to walk in your paths of kindness, peace, and justice.

Heavenly Father, out of love for me You have sent Jesus to be my Savior. I am thankful for that, and I want to show my love for You by loving my neighbor. Keep me from harming anyone by hand, mouth, heart, or mind. Help me to bear patiently the wrongs that others do to me. Grant me a forgiving heart that I may not try to gain revenge. Let no angry thoughts arise in my mind, and guard my tongue from angry words.

Fill my heart with love for my Savior that I may show love to others by being kind and helpful to them. Help me to be a good example to others, and use my good example to bring honor and praise to Your name and good to my friends and neighbors. Take us all to heaven in Your own good time.

Grant these blessings for the sake of Jesus. Amen.

—TEENAGERS PRAY

Prayer for Love of Neighbor

*W*hen neighbors don't measure up to our expectations, we can go to God for a change of heart. With his example and assistance, we can love our neighbors as God wants us to.

A Prayer for Allegiance to God

Deliver me, O God, from a slothful mind, from all lukewarmness, and all dejection of spirit. I know these cannot but deaden my love to you; mercifully free my heart from them, and give me a lively, zealous, active, and cheerful spirit, that I may vigorously perform whatever you command, thankfully suffer whatever you choose for me, and be ever ardent to obey in all things your holy love.

—JOHN WESLEY

Unfair

Life's not fair, and I stomp my foot in
frustration. The powerful get more while the
rest of us shrink, dreams for peace are shattered
while bullies get the upper hand, and despair is
as tempting as an ice cream sundae.
        Help me hold on, for you are a
        God of justice and dreams.

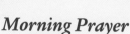

Morning Prayer

Bless us, Lord, as we go to worship this
morning. Look down upon our efforts to honor
        your name through song and word and
fellowship. And help us do it. For only in your
power do we live and move. And in your being
        alone do we find our true identity.

Lord, you love me with a faithful love, even when I am unfaithful. May your patience and grace give me confidence and joy, and may I love others as you have loved me.

Seeking
God's Grace and
Mercy

*H*ave mercy on me, O God,
have mercy on me,
for in you my soul takes refuge.
I will take refuge in the shadow
of your wings
until the disaster has passed.
I cry out to God Most High,
to God, who fulfills his
purpose for me.
He sends from heaven
and saves me,
rebuking those who hotly
pursue me;
God sends his love and
his faithfulness.

—PSALM 57:1–3 NIV

Continuing Grace

Give me a hint, steadfast God, about what lies ahead, for I want to see around the corner to the future. If that's not possible, help me live as if the future is now, assured that each day's grace will be sufficient.

A Healing Prayer

Only by calling on God for help are we able to truly forgive and forget.

Father, we praise you for your healing mercy. Thank you for loving and accepting us with all our hurts, hangups and sins, but thank you even more for caring enough to change us. Thank you for saving us from ourselves and our unwittingly self-destructive tendencies. We reach out and open up to receive your tender mercies, praising you for showing us that we are forgiven so that we may be able to forgive—both ourselves and others! Amen.

—JON EARGLE, *HEALING WHERE YOU HURT ON THE INSIDE*

River and Sky

Move our hearts with the calm, smooth flow of your grace. Let the river of your love run through our souls. May my soul be carried by the current of your love, towards the wide, infinite ocean of heaven.

Stretch out my heart with your strength, as you stretch out the sky above the earth. Smooth out any wrinkles of hatred or resentment. Enlarge my soul that it may know more fully your truth.

—GILBERT OF HOYLAND

Promise Keeper

*I*t's not always easy to be second. The second child gets hand-me-downs. The second chair in the orchestra is second fiddle. Hagar, the Egyptian girl in the Bible, had the unfortunate position of being second wife, a concubine in a culture where women were already second class.

She was a slave girl, and she belonged to Abraham's wife, Sarah. After years of trying to have a son, Sarah finally sent Hagar to Abraham's tent, unwilling to wait for God to keep his promise of an heir.

This did elevate Hagar's status, however. Perhaps Abraham liked her and sent for her again and again. But the Bible says she began to despise her mistress, especially after becoming pregnant.

Sarah didn't like this new arrangement. She gave Abraham an ultimatum: "It's her or me." Abraham chose Sarah. She was a beautiful woman, so beautiful that two kings tried to take her from him. And besides, they had been through a lot together, years of looking for a place of promise and waiting for a son. So he said to Sarah, "It's up to you. Do whatever you think is best." Sarah began to put Hagar in her place. She mistreated her. She may have even beat her. She certainly made her a slave again; we can be sure there was no place for her in Abraham's tent. So Hagar ran away.

Since she was an Egyptian, Hagar headed out across the wilderness in the direction of Egypt, along the road to Shur. But she didn't get very far. It was hot, she was weak, and she apparently collapsed beside a spring in the desert.

We can imagine that her prayer was very similar to the one we all pray at a time like that. The psalmist put it this way: "Turn to me and be gracious to me, for I am lonely and afflicted. Relieve the troubles of my heart, and bring me out of my distress."

It was there that an angel of the Lord appeared to her. "Where are you coming from, and where are you going?" he asked.

"I'm running away," she said.

The angel told her that wasn't a very good idea. "You are going to have a son," he said. "Go back home, and God will take care of you and bless you."

Alone in the desert, Hagar discovered a great truth: "I have now seen the one who sees me." And then she called the oasis where the angel appeared "A Well of the Living One Who Sees Me."

Hagar returned to Abraham, who loved her and their son. And later, when Sarah had a son of her own and sent Hagar away, God heard Hagar pray again and brought her to another well in the wilderness.

He kept his promise to her, as he does to us. He is the God who sees us and hears us, and shows us mercy, even when—or perhaps especially when—we are lonely and depressed.

Lord, let me bask in your awesome love. Let me rest in your presence. I've been away, like the prodigal son, wasting my life in selfish pursuits. But now I'm back, longing to be held in your loving arms. Forgive me, I pray, and welcome me back into your presence. Let me feel the dazzling warmth of your smile, and delight in your attention. Teach me your wisdom, show me your way, share with me your wants. Remind me again of who I am—and whose I am. In devoted love, Amen.

Lord, I confess to you, sadly
   my sin;
all I am, I tell to you, all I
   have been.
Purge all my sin away,
wash clean my soul this day;
Lord, make me clean.
Then all is peace and light this
   soul within;
thus shall I walk with you,
   loved though unseen.
Leaning on you, my God,
guided along the road,
nothing between!

—HORATIUS BONAR

Forgiveness

*Let me know the satisfaction of
forgiving today, O Lord. I have held
my peace and doused my anger. Now it is time
to extend my hand as you have to me.*

Discovery

O God, I am guilty of transgressions
that make me ashamed, and I fear you'll leave
me. Yet, have you ever refused to forgive those
who ask? Why would I be different?
Reassured, I accept forgiveness and will
share it with those who need it from me.

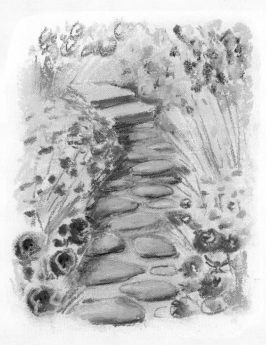

A Forgiving People

*V*ictor Hugo's classic tale *Les Miserables* testifies to the power of forgiveness. Early in the story, Jean Valjean is forgiven for stealing silver from a bishop, and he's given a chance to start a new life. He never forgets it as he grows into an influential businessman. Through the rest of his life he displays a giving, forgiving spirit.

It's a fact: Forgiven people forgive others. Jesus even put this principle in the Lord's Prayer—"Forgive us our debts, as we also have forgiven our debtors" (Matthew 6:12). Receive the forgiveness God grants you and then extend that mercy to others.

Releasing My Fears

*S*eeking courage, Lord, I bundle
my fears and place them in your hands.
Too heavy for me, too weighty even to ponder in
this moment, such shadowy terrors shrink to
size in my mind and—how wonderful!—
wither to nothing in your grasp.

Prayer for Healing Squabbles

*W*e come, needing your help to move beyond: the times we hurt one another; the times we willingly misunderstand, cherishing our differences; and the times we assume we know all there is to know about each other and turn away. And then there are the times that we make private rules only to publicly condemn anyone who fails to abide by them, limiting one another by labeling, interpreting, conditioning, insisting, resisting, and defining. From all this, Lord, we come, asking that you forgive us as we forgive those "others." We need new eyes to see and ears to hear. Be with us as we do so.

Revenge

*W*e know that revenge will settle nothing at this point. It will only leave us with an emptier feeling than before. Heal the pain in our hurts over this injustice, and somehow, as impossible as it now seems, bring us to the place of blessing our enemies and extending the one thing that keeps saving our own lives: your life-changing forgiveness.

Help for the Brokenhearted

*I*f anyone ever had a broken spirit, it was David, King of Israel.

He was a tough king in a rough world. In fact, God wouldn't allow him to build the temple because he was a man of war. His kingdom was filled with violence and sorrow. His own son rebelled and tried to take over his kingdom. And yet, David wrote many touching and thoughtful psalms, and his spirit was soft toward God. In fact, the Scriptures even call him a "man after God's own heart."

He had been a devout young man, who found both strength and solace in prayer. But as a mighty warrior and a young king, he became arrogant and selfish until his heart was broken, and then he returned to God.

The transformation occurred when he sent his troops off to war. He should have gone with them, for alone in the safety of his palace he saw and then seduced Bathsheba, the wife of one of his soldiers. Then, to cover his sins, he sent orders for her husband to be sent into the front lines to be killed.

The Lord sent the prophet Nathan to confront the young king, accusing him of both adultery and murder. "I have sinned against the Lord," David grievously admitted.

"Even so, the son born to you will die," the prophet said.

Sure enough, the baby that had been born to David and Bathsheba became sick, and David spent seven days fasting and praying for the child. David refused to eat or even bathe. Finally, when the baby died, he got up, washed himself, and worshiped the Lord.

There is no trace of bitterness in his response in a prayer of confession and faith recorded in Psalm 51. He acknowledged his sin, and he asked for forgiveness. And although he could not get his child back, he could get his joy back. "Restore to me the joy of your salvation, and sustain in me a willing spirit," he prayed. "My tongue will sing aloud of your deliverance. O Lord, open my lips, and my mouth will declare your praise" (Psalm 51:12, 14–15).

Because of his troubles David understood better who God was and what God wanted. "For you have no delight in sacrifice," he wrote. "The sacrifice acceptable to God is a broken spirit; a broken and contrite heart, O God, you will not despise" (Psalm 51:16–17).

David was still a man of war, a king with many challenges to confront. But he was a kinder and gentler king. Psalm after psalm reflects how in difficulty after difficulty he turned to God. "When the righteous cry for help, the Lord hears, and rescues them in their troubles," he writes. For David, this was especially true for the wounded and broken in spirit.

David believed God would comfort them, as he had comforted David himself beside the deathbed of his son. That is not to say there would be no consequences for their actions— but there would be mercy and forgiveness and strength.

That's just exactly what we need to be, men and women "after God's own heart."

My Mother Died

I don't belong to anyone now, Lord. My mother died today. Who will recall the stories of my birth? My first loose tooth? First day of school? Who will tell me I'm special, perfect, and always welcome me no matter what?

Reach out to me, a little child again, lost and frightened and suddenly orphaned. I'm no more than a marionette holding my own strings, no one on the other end. Stay with me until I fall asleep and be here should I awake, frightened. Let me be a child tonight. Tomorrow I'll be strong as befitting the new matriarch of this family. But for now, Lord, find me and hold me.

Man of Sorrows

Man of Sorrows, see my grieving heart this day. Keep me from feelings of shame, though, as I let the loss wash over me. For this is a part of my life, too, the life only you could give me: to learn what it means to let go.

Rainbow of Confession

*W*e're stained, like a paint rag, by troubles we caused ourselves, Lord. Red, the color of lost temper and rudeness. Green, envy of others who have it easier and more of it. Blue, the shade of despair over something we could change. Yellow, of cowardly running.

Rearrange our unsightly smudges into glorious rainbows through your divine gift of forgiveness.

Healing Failure

I blew it. Give me courage to admit my mistake, apologize, and go on. Keep me from getting stuck in denial, despair, and, worst of all, fear of trying again. In your remolding hands, God of grace, failures can become feedback and mistakes can simply be lessons in what doesn't work. Remind me that perfection means "suited to the task," not "without mistakes." There's a world of difference.

Our Provider

*Bless this food. And let it remind us once again
that the soul, like the body, lives and grows by
everything it feeds upon. Keep us drinking in
only the good and the pure, for your glory.
Through this meal, renew, refresh, and
revitalize both our bodies and our spirits by
reminding us that you are the one who sustains
us in every way. Amen.*

*Lighten our darkness, Lord, we pray; and in
your mercy defend us from all perils and
dangers of this night; for the love of your only
Son, our Savior Jesus Christ. Amen.*

—GELASIAN SACRAMENTARY,
"AN EVENING PRAYER"

Remember me, O Lord, but let's
Ignore my adolescent crimes.
Remember me, but please forget
The errors of my earlier times.
The blood of Christ can cover up
My callow deeds of waste and
    want.
I trust you, Lord, to overlook
The wrongs I've done that haze
    and haunt
My days and nights. Forgive
    my sin,
Turn wrong to right, and teach
    my soul
Your easy peace. Enfold me in
Your awesome love, and take
    control.

Forget my sins, but when you see
Me praying, Lord, remember *me*.

Reflections of Light

*H*eld up to your light, our broken hearts can become prisms that scatter micro-rainbows on the wall. Our pain is useless as it is, redeeming God, just as a prism is a useless chunk of glass until light passes through it. Remind us that the smallest ray of sun in a shower can create a rainbow. Use our tears as the showers and your love as the sun. Looking up, we see the tiniest arches of hope in the lightening sky.

Lost and Found:
A Sign of Hope to Follow

*D*aily stresses disorient me as completely as a red-winged blackbird, herald of spring, lost during an unexpected snowstorm. I am found, Lord, when I see your fingerprint in the whorls of a fern unfurling, lacy green and bold in the snow, and know that you are in charge, that you persevere, and that I, in you, can too. Then I know I was never lost at all, just a bit off-course like a wandering bird.

*T*urn to me and be
gracious to me,
for I am lonely and afflicted.
Relieve the troubles of my heart,
and bring me out of my distress.

—Psalm 25:16–17

Free Love

You love us, Lord, not because we are
particularly loveable. And it's certainly not the
case that you need to receive our love. I am so
heartened by this: You offer your love simply
because you delight to do it.

In His Hands

These are mean-spirited times, and we quake
and shudder. Tend us, loving Creator, and
shelter us in the palm of your hands against all
that would uproot and destroy us. We are the
flowers of your field.

·

Lord, I'm glad you are merciful and
gracious. Today I'm resting in your steadfast
love and in your arms. Amen.

Birds of a Feather

*T*roubles, dear Lord, have cast us loose from assumptions and certainties, and we are bobbing like rudderless boats on a stormy surf. When all hope seems gone, we spot doves on the horizon. Doves like those you sent Noah to assure him the Flood was nearly over. Such doves are in the phone calls from friends; in the smile of a neighbor; in the wisdom of a caregiver and counselor; in a hearty laugh or good, cleansing tears; in the flash of a new idea, a goal, and a dream.

We recognize landmarks now and can see our way through the storm, guided by your love-winged messengers.

God's Mercy

Finally, I've emerged from the dark night. Into the light with new energy, renewed vigor, and a body that responds again. Thank you for recovery and wholeness. And bless me as I tell others how good you are!

I Did It!

O Lord, I savor this triumph: I met my goal! Day by day, I reached into my heart and found energy to keep on. Day by day, I reached out and found your hand leading, your inspiration guiding, and your mercy and your grace.

*Lord, I know you are there,
even when I can't see you or feel
your presence. Bring me through
the darkness into the light and
make me a wellspring of joy
in the lives of others.*

A Closer Walk
With God

Today First

*I*n this time of change, help me
be patient, God. Let me not run
ahead of you and your plans.
Give me courage to do only what
is before me and to keep my
focus on my responsibilities.
I am tempted to daydream about
the future; however, the future is
in your hands. Thus, may I be
close to you in all my thoughts,
accomplish the task
before me today, and do it
with all my heart.

*Thank you, Lord, for holding my hand as I
take the next step in my journey forward.*

To be with God, there is no
need to be continually in church.
We may make [a chapel] of our
heart wherein to return from
time to time to converse with
him in meekness, humility, and
love. There is not in the world a
kind of life more sweet and
delightful than that of
a continual conversation
with God.

—BROTHER LAWRENCE

A Nudge From God

*Like an itch that won't let up, a buzz of
creativity is catching my attention and wanting
release. Help me recognize your presence in
this nudge to movement.*

Simply Sitting

O God, my days are frantic dashes between have to, ought, and should. There is no listening bone in me. Lead me to a porch step or a swing, a chair or a hillside where I can be restored by sitting, Lord, simply sitting. With you there to meet me, sitting places become prime places for collecting thoughts and restoring fragmented lives.

Sound Sleepers

Security, living God, is going to sleep in the assurance that you know our hearts before we speak and are waiting, as soon as you hear from us, to transform our concerns into hope and action, our loneliness into companionship, and our despair into dance.

In Stillness

I know that faith is what keeps me moving forward. But sometimes, my trust allows a leisure like this. For you, God, are the one who upholds all things. Even as I sit here in stillness, your breath keeps me breathing, your mind keeps me thinking, your love keeps me enjoying the life you've given me.

Be glad for all God is planning for you. Be patient in trouble, and always be prayerful.

—ROMANS 12:12 (NLT)

Holy God, you have shown me
   light and life.
You are stronger than any
   natural power.
Accept the words from my heart
That struggle to reach you,
Accept the silent thoughts and
   feelings
That are offered to you.
Clear my mind of the clutter of
   useless facts.
Bend down to me, and lift me in
   your arms.
Make me holy as you are holy.
Give me a voice to sing of your
   love to others.

—ANCIENT CHRISTIAN PRAYER,
   WRITTEN ON PAPYRUS

I praise you, for I am fearfully
and wonderfully made.
Wonderful are your works;
that I know very well.
My frame was not hidden
from you,
when I was being made in secret,
intricately woven in the
depths of the earth.
Your eyes beheld my
unformed substance.
In your book were written all the
days that were formed for me,
when none of them as
yet existed.

—PSALM 139:14–16

God Knows Me, Loves Me

The scope of Psalm 139 is as broad as the horizon and as personal as his concern for a newborn baby. Take time to read the psalm, and discover a God who cares for you.

I once went on a five-day retreat to a small hermitage run by a couple who would oversee my time of prayer and reflection. I moved into the trailer nestled deep in the woods on their property. I was excited and a little scared to have five days to myself, by myself. I had brought many books to read, and I had some ideas for projects that I might work on. The first night there, Ron came to talk to me about my plans for the retreat. I told him about what I intended to read and do. He gently suggested that I might want to set all the plans aside for the first day and just spend some time reading Psalm 139. I was open to the possibility, though I wanted to get on with my agenda. Ron suggested I be open to God's agenda.

In the morning, I decided to take a walk to check out my new surroundings, eat a leisurely breakfast, and then read Psalm 139 before

moving on to my other tasks. I never made it to the other tasks that day, and I never read most of the books I had so carefully packed. I got caught up in God addressing me in Psalm 139.

God knows me so well. God knows "when I sit down and when I rise up" (Psalm 139:2). God knows my thoughts and is acquainted with all my ways (verses 2 and 3). God knew when I was being made in secret, knit together in my mother's womb (verses 13 and 15). I was overwhelmed with God's knowledge and presence in my life. I wanted to both praise God and hide from him.

I wanted to praise God for the wonder of my life. "I am wonderfully made." I could take a walk and marvel at the way my body moved, thrill at the sight of the tall pines, and wonder at the smell of the flowers along the trail. I could eat breakfast and enjoy the taste of orange juice; I could turn my head when I heard a peck at the window and discover a cardinal greeting me every morning (sometimes earlier than I wanted to awaken). The five senses are part of being "wonderfully made," and they bring joy to living. But I also wanted to hide from God.

I was a little ashamed to be known so well. I hadn't done anything drastically wrong, but the thought of God knowing all my thoughts, knowing all my words, and watching over all my actions was overwhelming. I was humbled, and I was glad Jesus told us that God is a forgiving God. Even as I was aware of my shortcomings, I was confronted and blessed by a God who knows me so well and still loves me.

There is no place we can go and be out of the presence of God. "Where can I flee from your presence? . . . If I take the wings of the morning and settle at the farthest limits of the sea, even there your hand shall lead me, and your right hand shall hold me fast" (verses 7,

9–10). The images are so powerful so comforting. Even before we are born, we are known by God and held in God's heart. Humans are wonderfully made, and God looks out for our well-being.

I take a walk most mornings. Most people in the neighborhood probably think that I do it for the dog that accompanies me, but I really do it for me. I want to begin each day gently and quietly, so I can sense once again the presence of God. I can read about God's right hand holding me and about being made by God, but I want to open myself to remembering and experiencing the presence and love of God. As I walk, I say, "New is your love every morning, great God of light, and all day long you are working for good in the world. Stir up in us a desire to serve you, to live peacefully with our neighbors, and to devote each day to your Son, our Savior, Jesus Christ the Lord. Amen."

The prayer adjusts my focus for the day and puts me in touch with God and God's desire to be present in all the activities of my day. I return home from the walk a little better prepared for the day.

The psalmist reminds us that it is not only our personal efforts that keep us open to God, but also that God is continually seeking to be present with us. "Wonderful are your works, that I know very well." You do not have to read many psalms to know that creation is one of the ways that God is present to us. The stars, the sun, the trees, indeed, even the "heavens are telling the glory of God" (Psalm 19:1). The glories of creation not only point us toward the Creator, but they also become metaphors for our spiritual journey. The fast moving stream reminds me of how fast my life is going, and that I need to find still waters for rest. The winter trees remind me that even in emptiness work is being done to prepare for the spring. The beauty inside a tulip calls me to look deep inside myself and others for the traces of God's gifts. These works of God are wonderful teachers.

I don't remember the books I took with me on that retreat, but I do remember and hold precious Psalm 139 and commend it to you for your journey into the presence of God.

Lord, I feel so alone without you. Help me draw near to you and know the wonder of your loving presence. Thank you for never abandoning me and for allowing me to experience your presence.

A Room for Prayer

Jesus instructs us on letting go of distraction and entering a holy space for prayer. Worship is important: the gatherings of the community of faith for encouragement and comfort. Service is important: living out our faith. Yet worship and the life of faithful actions are knit together and undergirded with personal prayer, with a personal relationship with God. Jesus says, "Shut the door and spend some time with God."

Jesus is not saying you can pray only in your room with a closed door, but he uses the images to call us to set aside a time and a place for personal prayer. Where is your quiet place to pray? What is the best time for you to pray? When you are fresh and alert? Where can you close the door on the distractions of life? I have developed a practice of going over to an empty sanctuary and spending an hour in prayer before I sit at my desk to take care of the needs of the day. Others have a special room for meditation. Still others take a walk. More important than where we pray, Jesus is saying take time for prayer.

He is also saying we should prepare an "inner room" for prayer. Close the door to worry and to fear. A friend once said, "Anything worth worrying about is worth praying about." Close the door to being guarded in prayer or censoring what you think God can handle. Shut the door of the mind on mental distractions and just be with God. Still the body and quiet the mind, and spend time with God, who truly loves you.

*W*henever you pray, go into your
room and shut the door and pray
to your Father who is in secret.

—MATTHEW 6:6

*L*oving God, I place all my names before you.
Let me hear your voice calling me. Let me
know your embrace loving me. Let me feel your
power strengthening me. Let me experience
your calm chasing away my fears. Loving God,
I open myself to your love. Amen.

—LARRY J. PEACOCK, *WATER WORDS*

A Prayer Primer

*W*e accept your invitation to pray without
ceasing. Hear us as we pray boldly with
expectation, believing your assurance that we
deserve to be in your presence and to talk all we
want. We are grateful that you welcome us at
all times and in all places and moods.

Why Am I Here?

I come to church today, not because of duty
or because a preacher calls, but because you,
O God, invite me, your child, for whom you've
been searching. In the words and songs, the
lights and symbols, I feel your Spirit,
like a pulse, beating within me.

Prayer for a Renewed Heart

Today I want to spend time with you, God. In fact, I'd like to spend the whole day just being in your presence. For this one day, I will not worry about the work I have to do or the goals I want to accomplish. I will pull back and simply listen for your guidance.

I'm willing to change my life in order to fit your perfect will, and I ask that you begin that work in my heart, even now. I'll let go of personal ambition for you. I'll loosen my grip on the things I've wanted to accomplish and the recognition I've craved for so long. All of this I give over to you.

I'm content to be a servant, quiet and unnoticed, if that is what you desire for my life. I'm even willing to be misunderstood by others, if you will only respond to my sincere prayer for a renewed heart. I need to be in the center of your will. Always.

Jesus, Thou Joy of Loving Hearts

Jesus, Thou Joy of loving hearts,
Thou Fount of life, Thou Light
   of men,
From the poor bliss that earth
   imparts,
We turn unfilled to Thee again.

Thy truth unchanged hath ever
   stood;
Thou savest those that on
   Thee call;
To them that seek Thee Thou art
   good,
To them that find Thee all in all.

We taste Thee, O Thou living Bread,
And long to feast upon Thee still;
We drink of Thee, the Fountainhead,
And thirst our souls from Thee
   to fill.

Our restless spirits yearn for thee,
Wherever our changeful lot is cast;
Glad when Thy gracious smile we see,
Blessed when our faith can hold
   Thee fast.

O Jesus, ever with us stay,
Make all our moments calm and
   bright,
Chase the dark night of sin away,
Shed over the world Thy holy light.

—St. Bernard of Clairvaux

At Home With God

Sidetracked, lost, and wandering far from the home of the heart, I long to be at home with you. Home, not so much a place as a togetherness where I am loved and welcomed just as I am, where I am sheltered, nourished, and equipped. Indeed, I get a glimpse of being at home with you, God, when I am being constantly nurtured by an ever-present, always-loving parent.

Familiar Words,
Wonderful Promises

For many people, myself included, the first Bible verse ever memorized was John 3:16: "For God so loved the world that he gave his only Son, so that everyone who believes in him may not perish but may have eternal life." I can remember sitting in the basement of my church trying to memorize various Bible verses, but the one that remains is John 3:16. It is such a pivotal verse in the Bible and seems to have entered American culture as a summary of Christian faith. Often at a sporting event, you can see someone holding up a sign with just the words: "John 3:16." The verse seems to be everywhere, but its familiarity should not cause us to lose regard for its significance.

The verse is part of a dialogue between Jesus and a Pharisee named Nicodemus, a leader of the Jews. The dialogue is held in the quiet of the night, perhaps so Nicodemus won't be seen going to Jesus. Yet, he is genuinely interested in the message that Jesus has been teaching. The dialogue takes different twists and leaves Nicodemus wondering about how to be born from above, how to be born anew. Jesus is taking Nicodemus into deeper understandings of faith and life. It is not so much the physical that can be seen, but the spiritual, which is invisible, and yet, still is as noticeable as the wind. Jesus invites Nicodemus to be aware of the movement of the Spirit and to receive its insights.

Jesus is pointing Nicodemus and us to the incredible love of God—a love so big it reaches out to embrace the whole world and a love so deep that God is willing to send his son to show us salvation.

This is a passage about love and God's intentions that all might be saved, that all might know the tender embrace of God in life and in life beyond death. But we must read the verse that follows. Frequently it seems as though we have forgotten to also read verse 17: "God did not send the son into the world to condemn the world." It is so easy to be judgmental and critical. It is so easy to point out another person's faults, another nation's errors. We should ask one another's forgiveness for losing track of the central theme of God's love—God was willing to let Jesus die so we might see the power of sacrificial love.

In Jesus' death and resurrection, he became the risen Christ, who is not bound by human limitations but is free to be known in all times and places. The risen Christ shows us the path to eternal life.

Several years ago, while on a wilderness prayer retreat, I talked with Christ, and I felt as though Christ knew my struggles and questions. I heard words of reassurance: "I know what you are going through. None of us received all the love we needed from our parents. I will be with you. I am as close to you as your breath." The conversations renewed a relationship with Jesus, who is still present to us as the risen Christ, crossing all boundaries of time and space. Such moments in prayer are a foretaste of eternal life, which is present in our daily lives if we but look. The communion with Christ is a taste of what is to come, for neither life nor death, nor things present, nor things to come can separate us from the love of God in Christ Jesus our Lord (see Romans 8:31–39).

Indeed, John 3:16–17 serves as an important reminder that God's will is for all people to come into a relationship with God. Jesus is the avenue to that homecoming; the risen Christ is the pathway to eternal life. St. Augustine said it wisely, "Our hearts are restless till they find their rest in God."

Thank you, Lord,
that you are our resting place
for our weary hearts.

Assurance

*I*n a world of fickle loyalties and unkept promises, we can count on you, our "no matter what" God. Like a roof, you are over our heads, sheltering us. Like the horizon, your life-changing power stretches beyond us, and like water in the rivers, oceans, and the essence of life that flows through our veins, you are within us. Most of all, no matter what distracts and tempts us, we know that, like fish in the sea, we are in you.

Signs of Hope

*W*e know you, Lord, in the changing seasons: in leaves blazing gently in fall beauty and in winter's snow sculptures. We know you in arid desert cactus bloom and in migration of whale and spawn of fish and turtle. In the blending of the seasons, we feel your renewing, steadfast care, and worries lose their power to over-whelm. The list of your hope-filled marvels is endless.

You are everywhere, Lord, comforting
and guiding us as we move through life's
extremes. You are with us in birthings
and dyings, in routine and surprise, and
in stillness and activity. We cannot
wander so far in any direction that you
are not already there with us.

O Lord, be my home. Let me rest in you, live in you, and come home to you. I want to abide in your love. Write your commandments on my heart so my greatest desire is to honor you with my life. As I work and play, as I talk and pray, surround all my doings with your energizing presence. In your holy name, I pray.

Silent Prayer

Bless me with silent conversations, O God, so I may be with you while doing chores, while singing in the shower, and while driving the car. Sometimes words don't have to be spoken to be understood, and I get your message, too, in the silence that fills and comforts.

Goodness of God

We spend a lot of time as prospectors of truth, digging, sifting, discarding the world's "fool's gold" that is so lovely and enticing. You, O God, are the genuine article. Bless us with the power to go into our daily lives energized by this truth and equipped to transform our searching world.

Because of You

Lord of my heart, give me a refreshing drink from the fountain of your love, walking through this desert as I have. Lord of my heart, spread out before me a new vision of your goodness, locked into this dull routine as I was. Lord of my heart, lift up a shining awareness of your will and purpose, awash in doubts and fears though I be.

A Christmas Prayer

*T*he Christmas tree, O God, is groaning beneath gift-wrapped anticipation. The table spread before us is resplendent with shared foods prepared by loving hands, for which we give thanks.

And now, as this waiting season ticks to a bell-ringing, midnight-marvelous close, we around this table are moving over to make room for the anticipated Guest. Come, bless us with the gift of your presence as we say, "Welcome."